Legal Almanac Series No. 74

FINDING
THE
LAW
A GUIDE TO LEGAL RESEARCH

by   David Lloyd, J.D.
Law Librarian
J. Reuben Clark Law School
Brigham Young University

1974 OCEANA PUBLICATIONS, INC.
Dobbs Ferry, New York

This is the seventy-fourth in a series of LEGAL ALMANACS
which bring you the law on various subjects in nontechnical
language. These books do not take the place of your attorney's
advice, but they can introduce you to your legal rights and
responsibilities.

Library of Congress Cataloging in Publication Data

Lloyd, David, 1946-
    Finding the law.

    (Legal Almanac series, no 74)
    Includes bibliographies.
    1. Legal research--United States. I. Title.
KF240.L59   340'.07'2073   74-10762
ISBN 0-379-11090-3

/

Manufactured in the United States of America

TABLE OF CONTENTS

FOREWORD

Finding the Law is an elementary book aimed at assisting first-year law students and novices in the law to use the law library on a very basic level. There are other books on legal bibliography that are much more detailed, but require much more time in reading to understand the legal research system. For questions unanswered by this book, more detailed books should be consulted.

This book is a companion book to another Oceana Publications Inc. Legal Almanac Series publication: Roy M. Mersky, Law Books for Non-Law Libraries and Laymen, A Bibliography. Legal Almanac Series No. 44. 1969. Professor Mersky's book should be used with this book by students in a general library.

There is nothing mysterious about the laws of the United States. The American system of law is based upon long traditions of common law that developed from the needs of the peoples of England. We have also borrowed the best laws and customs from other historic legal systems, including the Roman civil law, the Greek laws, and the Judeo-Christian heritage. Many laws are common-sense interpretations of justice and fair play. These common law rules are the basis of the complex and sophisticated laws necessary in the modern industrial state. Because of the complexity of the many laws, court decisions, and regulations that have grown out of the rapid industrialization of our society, law books have proliferated at an extraordinary rate. It is because of this rapid growth in the number of specialized law books that a book such as this is necessary for laymen and beginning law students. By carefully following the rules in this book, the reader may research and fully understand any doctrine of law.

I am grateful for the comments of the first-year law students in the Charter Class of the J. Reuben Clark Law School who used the first half of this book as their text for legal bibliography. I am also grateful to Professors Robert L. Schmid, George S. Grossman, and Roy M. Mersky, to whom I am indebted for teaching me the principles of legal research and legal bibliography. This book is for Davy and Wendy. I am indebted to my secretary, Ms. Linda Harries, and my research assistant, Mr. Thomas E. Barzee, Class of 1976, for their work on the manuscript.

Chapter 1

INTRODUCTION TO LAW

1 THE LAW SYSTEM

1.1 People tend to view law as a criminal justice system, or the divorce court, or a deficit federal budget, or a traffic ticket, or a title search on a new home; they do not view it from the same perspective as the lawyer, who must see it as a unified system based upon a complex structure of interrelated rules, procedures, and proscriptions. Law works as the regulating force of society. Though at times clumsy and unwielding, it nevertheless serves as the cohesive structure around which all other pursuits must gather. One need only look at the vast, complex society in which we live to appreciate laws controlling traffic on freeways or on crowded city streets, regulations prohibiting two television stations from transmitting on channel 2, a semi-operative crime control system that slows the rate of violent crimes, rules governing the transfer of goods and services over long distances, and freedom from arbitrary governmental snooping on personal lives.

1.2 The American law system consists of a vast, intertwining network of laws, judicial decisions, regulations, executive orders, treaties, discretionary rulings, and constitutions and common law steeped in tradition. At the head of the legal system is the charter (Constitution) granted to government by the people -- in whom exists all of the source of law and power. The Constitution is a grant of power, but it is a limited grant of power. The people reserved some power to the state governments (which they also created) and the remainder to themselves and their posterity. Early in American history, the Supreme Court declared itself the guardian of the people's charter and commenced upon a course that led to the judicial declaration of unconstitutionality of unauthorized Congressional and state actions. The only major constitutional crisis -- e.g., when government or men usurped powers not granted by the people -- was the Civil War. Since that time there has been a constant struggle over allocations of power between the national government, the states, and the people, but this struggle has not reached crisis proportions.

The Constitution is the supreme law of the land, and all laws, rules, actions and judgments to the contrary are null and of no force -- in theory.

1.3 What is law, then? Viewed in its broad perspective, it is the fabric of social control. People respond to the social pressure created by the recognition of basic rules. The social pressure is backed by ultimate political force. The thread of law in the broader fabric of social control, is, of course, the aggregate of understood laws and legal precepts. But more narrow in scope is the fiber of the law structure -- the judicial process of conflict resolution. It is more at this "conflict resolution" level that lawyers become involved and the law begins to affect specific people. In the daily routine of law enforcement, trials, administrative hearings, and legislative actions, the reality of law as a function of social control is illustrated. This book is concerned with determining what occurs in this daily routine, what rules guide the actions in this routine, and what principles are to be employed. Overriding the control aspects of law are moral and philosophical considerations. These lurk throughout the law at every level -- and frequently are the final arbitrary foundation of public policy. In researching law topics, the implicit philosophical considerations (termed "jurisprudential considerations" by lawyers) may be difficult to ascertain, but frequently will provide the key to understanding the rule of law involved.

2 THE ROLE OF THE LAWYER

2.1 The basic role of the modern lawyer is to aid people who become embroiled in conflicts as well as to prevent future conflicts from developing through careful planning and drafting of documents. He must be able to sift the relevant facts from a client's case before preparation of a trial, a will, a corporate charter, a tax return, a deed, etc. He must have a competent knowledge of the rules of law and procedures. This general knowledge that the lawyer possesses enables him to research specific questions rapidly and logically. It is the lawyer's breadth of vision, analytical ability, and knowledge of the law that he sells as a service to his clients.

2.2 For the student about to begin legal research for the first time, the law library may seem to be an impenetrable jungle. Regardless of how mystical it may seem, however, the law library is, like the law and lawyers that it serves, highly organized, though complex. In order to understand what the law library is, the beginning student must first gain an appreciation of what lawyers do and what law is.

2.3 Contrary to popular notions, many lawyers do not spend much time in the courtroom practicing on behalf of a client. In fact, the lawyer spends a surprising amount of his time in a law library looking up the law on a particular point. When a lawyer receives facts from a client describing a dispute or involving planning for an estate, a property transaction, request for a license from one of the regulatory agencies of the federal government, or many other situations which lawyers are involved in, the lawyer sifts through those facts that he has received from the client and then searches out the applicable rules governing the relevant facts. He does this by using the law books in a law library.

2.4 Our legal system is based upon the English common law system of law. That is, unless one of the legislative bodies enacts a statute governing particular conduct or affairs, court judges will determine what is just and fair in a particular dispute, and, in thus determining what is fair in one circumstance, lay down a rule that can be followed in a later case involving similar facts and circumstances. The process of relying solely upon judge-made law or common law is being more and more supplemented by statutes from the fifty state legislatures, Congress, and regulations by administrative bodies, but it will never be replaced, because these statutes and regulations must be interpreted, and the decisions of the courts interpreting these statutes and regulations are also law.

2.5 Thus the laws are constantly changing, either through court decisions, new statutes and regulations, or court decisions interpreting statutes and regulations. It is the lawyer's task to determine, through use of the law library, what the current rules of law are on a given subject and then apply that law to the facts of the particular case that he is involved with.

2.6 What is the lawyer searching for? The attorney is looking for authority -- something that will convince the court before which he is practicing that the law should be as he argues it is. For example, Farmer Brown sells Happy Time Market a case of tomatoes. On the same day Bill, the stockboy, places the tomatoes on the display case only to find that all of the tomatoes under the top layer are rotten. Happy Time owner Bruno goes to his lawyer, Ray Zipsa, and demands satisfaction against Farmer Brown. Mr. Zipsa looks at the Uniform Commercial Code and finds that in a sale of goods there is an implied warranty of fitness -- and that the local supreme court has said that in a case involving rotten apples, the farmer had to refund the money or supply good apples, plus pay for any consequential damages. Relying on this statute and court decision, Ray Zipsa writes Farmer Brown a firm letter requesting a new carton of good tomatoes and money damages. When Farmer Brown refuses, Lawyer Zipsa goes into court and, on the basis of the rules expressed above, Judge Hardly issues an order requiring Farmer Brown to comply with Lawyer Zipsa's demands.

2.7 Mandatory Authority. Courts are obliged to follow the statutes properly passed by the legislative body that is the sovereign of that jurisdiction so long as they are constitutional, although a court may give a strict interpretation or meaning to the statute. In other words, for the state of Utah, the courts are bound to follow laws properly enacted by the Utah legislature unless the law is unconstitutional. Often, however, the statute, as strictly or narrowly applied, is not applicable, and the court is free to either interpret the statute broadly and make the statute cover the facts in the case or the court itself may pronounce a new rule of law, or judicial opinion, which then becomes binding authority on any lower courts. Once a rule has been stated, for example, by the Utah supreme court, or a statute is enacted, the lower courts in Utah, called trial courts or courts of original jurisdiction, must follow that rule of law until the holding is overruled by the supreme court, or until the statute is changed by the legislature, or the judicial decision is overruled in effect by the legislature's passing a statute stating a new rule covering the same circumstances. Normally when a court such as the Supreme Court of Utah has stated a rule, it will continue to follow that rule in later cases under the principle of stare decisis, which means that for various reasons, the court will always follow the rules that it has previously announced unless there are compelling reasons for changing those rules.

2.8 Persuasive Authority. There is another kind of authority, but it is merely persuasive authority. For example, a statute in Utah may be similar to a statute in California; in fact, the statute in Utah may have been copied from the California statute. If there have been no judicial decisions regarding the interpretation of the Utah statute, the court in Utah may be persuaded to look to the California court decisions to see what that court has done. The fact that the California supreme court has acted in one way may be persuasive to the Utah court and an attorney will want to find out what the California courts have said about a statute that Utah had copied. The decision in California, however, is <u>not binding</u> on the Utah court. Persuasive authority, then, merely persuades, it does not have the commanding effect that the sovereign has. It is persuasive because of the soundness of reasoning, the status of the court that rendered the decision in the jurisdiction, or the particular ability or recognized expertise of the author of a treatise or law review article. Thus it may tend to influence the court even though it is, of course, not binding on the court.

2.9 Decisions of the Supreme Court of the United States are binding upon all state and federal courts where the Court is interpreting federal legislation and the Constitution applicable to the states; but as to matters of local state law, the U.S. Supreme Court decision is only persuasive to the states' courts and not binding. Federal courts must follow state supreme court decisions where the federal court within a given state is determining a matter involving state law.

2.10 Persuasive authority includes judicial opinions from other jurisdictions, statutes from other jurisdictions, federal decisions, federal statutes, law review articles, legal treatises, legal encyclopedias, restatements of law, and other commentaries, depending upon the status of the author. Court decisions are binding in a later case only if the law is applicable to the particular set of facts in the case. The portion of the court decision that is binding is the "holding" of the court. Most cases involve a particular set of facts, and, while the rule of law announced by the court may be broad, the "holding" of the case is the law as applied to those facts, and nothing more. Anything that the court may say about the case is regarded as mere "dictum," and while it may have the force of law, it is merely the opinion of the author of the decision and is not really the binding holding of the court. However, common sense would indicate that when the court strongly mentions a particular matter in connection with a case, and there is no dissent, it may follow that suggestion in a later case involving facts that would fit within that dictum.

3 THE APPELLATE SYSTEM

3.1 One of the primary sources of law is the decisions of the courts, both state and federal. The lawyer is directly involved in the litigation process leading to court decisions. The judge is a neutral party in court proceedings -- the burden of going forward is always on the attorneys. When a trial is held, a judgment of some kind is made by the judge. He will be responsible for finding the appropriate facts (assisted by the jury if one is used), then he must apply the law to those facts. If the judge makes an error during the course of the trial, the losing party may ask the lawyer to have the error reviewed by a higher court. The procedure used to reach the higher court is an appeal. The higher court is thus termed an appellate court. A true appellate court reviews only the record or transcript of the trial court. It does not call any witnesses or admit any new evidence. The reviewing procedure consists of studying the written arguments of the opposing lawyers (called briefs) and listening to a short oral argument by each of the attorneys. The appellate court (normally three or more judges) will then deliberate and write an opinion listing its judgment and the reasons it has so ruled. Most reported court opinions are from appellate courts. Few trial opinions are recorded and published. The major exception is the published reports of the federal district courts -- the better opinions and more interesting cases are reported in the Federal Supplement. So, by and large, judicial decisions, accounting for about half of the law, consist of only those cases appealed to higher courts. A notorious case such as the Angela Davis trial in California is unreported because it was not appealed.

3.2 The Supreme Court of the United States is the most prestigious appellate court and its procedures for accepting cases are important. The Court has certain limited trial functions such as controversies between two states. It also hears cases on appeal, but the Congress has limited these cases. One basis of appeal is a state court declaration that a federal law is repugnant to the Constitution. The bulk of the Court's load are cases that it has discretion to hear. The complaining appellant files a petition for a writ of certiorari. If four or more members of the Court vote to hear the case, the writ is granted, briefs are submitted, and oral arguments presented. If less than four members of the Court decide to hear a case in which a petition for a writ of certioriari has been filed, it denies the writ. There are many reasons why the Supreme Court may decide to deny the writ -- so no conclusions should be formed. The importance of the denial of the writ of certiorari is simply that the lower court judgment is allowed to stand.

4 THE FEDERAL SYSTEM -- STATE V. NATIONAL GOVERNMENT

4.1 The highest court of each state is the final judge of matters over which the Supreme Court of the United States has

6

no jurisdiction. If there are no federal questions involved, or diversity of citizenship (of different states) -- there is no power in the U.S. Supreme Court to act.

4.2 There was a period of United States history when the Supreme Court of the United States assumed a superior role in the development of a "national common law." In cases where diversity of citizenship existed, the federal courts were free to determine which law should apply and what the law of the state of which the parties were domiciled should be. For a long period, the U.S. Supreme Court and the federal appeal courts played an important role in the shaping of a national body of common law. They ceased this activity in 1938, but the rise of the power of the national government assisted by concurrent Supreme Court decisions merely rechanneled federal supremacy. In addition to increased federal supremacy, the increase in nationalizing activities such as the growth of uniform laws and the restatements, and other attempts at codification tend to lessen the dramatic importance of state legislatures and courts, but state codes and court reports still represent the primary sources for legal research.

Chapter 2

RESEARCHING THE COMMON LAW

5 LOCATING THE CASE IN POINT

5.1 <u>Analysis of the Problem.</u> The starting point of any research should be a careful analysis of the facts involved, the solution to be sought and the method for achieving the solution. The simple facts of a given situation may result in several apparent legal wrongs -- the cure must also be reckoned with. For example, assume that <u>A</u> and <u>B</u> live next to a cement factory. <u>A</u> works in a nearby city. <u>A</u> has lived at his current residence for thirty years. <u>B</u> is a farmer. <u>B</u> owns and manages two hundred acres of prime farm land and raises crops and livestock. <u>B</u> has owned the farm for ten years. Twenty years ago the cement factory, C.F. Co., moved to its present location adjoining the property of <u>A</u> and <u>B</u>. It gradually grew in size until last year it was a major producer of cement in the Middle West. Business is very bright for C.F., which should place it in a position to expand its plant to double the capacity. <u>A</u> is tired of living in his present home and wants to sell. <u>A</u> been unsuccessful in his efforts to sell because he is offering it for much more than the current market price and also because people are reluctant to move next to the pollution and noise of the C.F. Co. plant. <u>B</u> is having a bad year generally and wants to retire while he still can salvage his equipment and remaining livestock. <u>B</u> hears of the expansion efforts of C.F. Co. and threatens to block them in court for ruining his farm unless they guarantee him an annual stipend of $2,000. <u>A</u> also hears of the expansion and threatens to sue C.F. Co. for medical bills on account of his son's coughing unless they purchase his home and lot. As the attorney for <u>A</u>, <u>B</u>, or C.F. Co., what are the rights of each party? This problem has been simplified because the facts are already ascertained. Normally the facts must be painfully pieced together through a long session with the client and the careful inquiries of the other parties. Now that the facts are known, what is wanted by the clients? Neither <u>A</u> nor <u>B</u> wants to see the plant closed down. They want money damages. C.F. Co. cannot afford to have the plant closed down. They have so far evaded pollution statutes and

8

they do not want to pay money damages.

5.2 Converting the Problem Analysis into Legal Terminology. Fact situations and desired solutions must be converted into legal terms so that the legal indexes may be used to locate legal precedent. Words and Phrases, a multivolume set located in many general libraries as well as law libraries, can be used to convert layman's language into legal terms. Case digests such as the West General Digest system or state digests also contain a "words and phrases" volume converting layman's language into legal terms. In the above example, a lawyer would know from experience that the cement plant problem will involve such legal concepts as nuisance, tort, environmental pollution, statute of limitations, consent, real property law, perhaps water rights, damages, etc. These key concepts can then be used to investigate further.

5.3 Pinpoint Topics to Be Searched. There are thousands of reported cases on nearly every major legal subject. Each major legal subject is subdivided into very narrow points of law -- but still with hundreds of cases on each narrow point. The trick to efficient legal research is in narrowing the search to avoid reading too many irrelevant cases. This is done through quickly scoping out the topic through the use of the legal encyclopedias such as Corpus Juris Secundum or American Jurisprudence, or using one of the smaller legal treatises such as one of the books in the Hornbook series, the Textbook series, or other short treatises such as those located at the reserve desk of any university law school library or at a county or bar association library. The same thing can be accomplished by looking carefully through the index to the subject at the beginning of each subject in the multivolume case digests. In any case, the object is to locate the ballpark and then zero in on the applicable doctrines until the subject is narrowed enough to find the particular cases needed to either be "in point" (directly applicable as legal precedent) or close enough to be useable as analogous situations and thus reliable for use as precedent.

5.4 Searching the Narrowed Topic. Once an isolated topic has been identified that should provide the rule of law governing a particular set of facts, the following steps should be useful.

5.4.1 If the topic was discovered in Corpus Juris Secundum (C.J.S.), quickly check the pocket supplement under the topic name and section number for any revisions or additional footnotes. For example, in C.J.S., volume 25, under the topic "Damages," § 27 discusses uncertainty as to the existence or cause and states the rule that recovery is not available unless actual damage can be shown with reasonable certainty. In the footnote to this statement, the editor has cited numerous court cases in an alphabetical listing of states. There is not a case holding this way cited for Maryland. A quick check in the supplement in the back of the book under footnote 5 reveals the citation to a recent Maryland case: Straughan v. Tsouvales, 228 A.2d 300, 246 Md. 242. The citation can then be used to locate the case. (See ¶ 6.1.5 infra.) A notation at the beginning of §27 states "Library Reference: Damages Key #6." With this reference and key number any state, regional, or general digest published by West Publishing Company can be used to broaden the search for cases. The topic in the digest system is also "damages," but the search number is West's own device, which is a number placed after a small key-shaped sign. In any West digest, the key #6 under the topic of "damages" will produce similar cases, and in the Maryland Digest, will produce the same case.

5.4.2 If American Jurisprudence 2d (Am.Jur.2d) was used, the narrow question of whether recovery can be had where it is uncertain whether the client suffered any damage is dealt with in §24 of the topic "Damages." The encyclopedia merely restates the rule. The particular cases are referenced by a footnote. In footnote 8, a list of cases is given as well as a citation to a longer discussion appearing in the set of annotated law reports, American Law Reports (ALR). A check of the supplement shows no additional cases on that rule of law.

5.4.3 If using a treatise, it will cite case law as well as discuss the general rules and philosophy behind the rule. As a general principle, it is nearly always better to begin searching for case law in an up-to-date treatise supplemented regularly if one is available. In the damages example above, §25 of McCormick on Damages explains the rule and traces its history and rationale. The footnotes cite cases as well as law review articles.

5.5 Broadening the Topic Search

5.5.1 After reviewing the general area of law through the use of the legal encyclopedias or treatises, an exhaustive case search must be made on each point of law. There are two basic methods that can be used: the West digest system or the American Law Reports system. A conscientious researcher will use both. The busy practicing lawyer will use the method he is used to using. Either method works well.

5.5.2 The digest system. All of the reported cases in the United States appear in the digest system. Cases are indexed

10

by name of case (Mueller v. Peterson) in both plaintiff tables (Mueller is the plaintiff) and in defendant tables (Peterson is the defendant, and in "defendant" tables would be listed first, in alphabetical order). Cases are also indexed by court. Federal cases are thus indexed in the Federal Digest and the later updated set, Modern Federal Practice Digest. U.S. Supreme Court cases are indexed in the Supreme Court Digest and the U.S. Supreme Court Digest, Lawyers Edition. Each state, except Utah, Nevada, and Delaware, has a separate state digest for the case law of that state. Each state law library will have the local state digest. Larger law libraries will have every state digest. The regional digests, which match the regional reporters, cover the cases for a geographical region. The most useful item in the regional digest is the index to cases in the corresponding regional reporter. The digest that reports all cases, both state and federal, is the American Digest System. Current cases are compiled in monthly pamphlets. Cases from the current blue, monthly pamphlets back to 1966 are in green, bound volumes called the General Digest. Thereafter, the Decennial Digests representing ten years of compiled General Digests work back to 1896. The cases reported during the period from 1658 to 1896 are covered by the Century Digest.

5.5.3 The digests are used primarily as a guide to various kinds of law subjects. Digests are limited to providing references to case law. Digests are not generally useful in providing any information about statutes and ordinances. The information appearing on a subject such as "adoption" in the digests is a simple restatement of one particular point of law appearing in a court opinion. The short statement appears in the "adoption" section because the summary of the statement of law appearing in the court opinion pertains to adoption. The entire court opinion may deal almost exclusively with another subject, such as "wills and trusts." Thus, while one now has a short statement of law on the topic of adoption, it may have little real value as legal authority or precedent. The digest contains many thousands of short summaries of statements of law on many topics. The simple fact that one case can only have one legal holding restricts the use of the short summary or "headnote" as it is called.

The case itself must be examined carefully to insure that the suspected meaning is the actual meaning in the context of the case opinion. The West American Digest System employs over 450 general subject headings, such as administrative law and procedure, adoption, armed services, aviation, bankruptcy, de-

11

claratory judgment, federal civil procedure, internal revenue, labor relations, mental health, social security and public welfare, telecommunications, trade regulations, and zoning. Each general topic begins with an outline analysis of the scope of the topic. At the end of each topic scope is a list of related topics to explore as well as references to legal encyclopedias and legal treatises. After each scope note analysis section in all of the West digests are the short summary headnotes. Each general area under the main topic is given a "key" number. For example in the American Digest System, "Adoption Key #1. Nature of the proceeding" contains U.S. Supreme Court headnotes, federal lower courts headnotes, and notes from the highest courts of each state, beginning with cases from Alabama to Wyoming, which discuss the general nature of adoption. Most of these headnotes mention that adoption is entirely a matter of legislation and statutory law, with citations to the page of a reporter where a court has made such a statement. This key number -- Adoption #1 -- can be used to transfer into any regional or state digest, or from these digests into the complete American Digest System.

The reason for using the state digest over the American Digest System is because of the clumsy nature of going through the separate multivolume compilations of the General Digest and pamphlets as well as the separate decennials. To effectively use the American Digest System, each separate volume in the General Digest portion (green books) must be searched under the topic and key number. The American Digest System is the only method, however, of insuring that all relevant American cases are searched.

5.5.4 Selecting the Relevant Headnotes. Cases (headnotes) are arranged chronologically in the digest. No attempt is made by the indexers to indicate the value of a case or to note that the case has been subsequently overruled by the same court or another court. The decisions that must be made as to the relative merits and value of a case cited in a headnote are entirely the responsibility of the researcher. Further, the headnote is only a clue to the language and context of the case cited. The headnote is a summary of a point of law extracted from a case by a professional indexer. The indexer's ability to properly interpret a case should never be relied upon by a researcher. The actual case must be read.

5.5.5 Searching with the American Law Reports. Many cases decided each year have little value to the researcher as authority simply because they duplicate points of law clearly established. Occasionally such cases present novel fact sit-

12

uations but on the whole represent stumbling blocks to quick research. Important cases -- those which are a departure from the previous law, or distinguish carefully the current law -- appear less frequently. These cases are published in the American Law Reports (A.L.R.). Along with each important case reported in full is a lengthy "annotation" -- a discussion by an editor of the area of law presented in the case. The annotation will include an overview of the subject area, conflicts between the jurisdictions, the questions yet unresolved, the history and basis of the legal rules presented, and citations to the reporters, encyclopedia (Am. Jr.), treatises, and law reviews.

5.5.6 How to Locate an A.L.R.Annotation. The quickest way to get into A.L.R. is to look for in-point annotations while reading through the general area of law in Am. Jr. (the legal encyclopedia). Otherwise, there is a complicated digest system, located usually with the three series of A.L.R., called A.L.R. Digests, and other finding devices. The Quick Index to A.L.R. 1st, 2nd, and 3d uses key words as an index and is the easiest beginning point. The annotations are indexed by subject and key words by editors who use an indexing method that must be converted into the researcher's language. The A.L.R. Digests are no more difficult to use than other digests and follow a subject approach with a table of cases. Converting layman's language into ALR Digest language is done with the word index called Quick Indexes. ALR Federal has a separate digest.

5.5.7 Updating the ALR Annotation. One of the very valuable services to ALR users is the annotation update service that provides comments supplementing or superseding earlier annotations. The Later Case Service volumes are indexed by volume and page number for the basic annotation being updated. ALR 3d is updated in pocket supplements to each volume. For example, an annotation on mental disease as a defense to tort liability may appear in an older volume of A.L.R. -- 26 A.L.R.230. The later case service note for 26 A.L.R. 230 may not only have new and recent information but also may cite several new annotations. Thus by having picked up the annotation citation in a case, law review article, brief, etc., the annotation can be quickly updated by using the Later Case Service. ALR 3d volumes are currently updated by pocket supplements. All annotations must be checked for current relevance through the update method. All cases found in ALR must be Shepardized like any other case.

5.5.8 Locating a Case -- Digest v. Annotated Reports. ALR and its indexes, including Am. Jr., are a good tool for busy practicing lawyers. Its annotations are frequently cited by courts. It is usually located together as one set and is physically easier to use; whereas, the reporter system involves a much larger storage area. The deficiency is the inability to cover all of the law and the probability of missing a later case. The digest system to the West reporters as well as the Corpus Juris Secundum provide more complete coverage of the case law so long as all possible subjects are checked to insure completeness. Often a point of law will be indexed by a not-so-obvious topic and subtopic key number. Thus in using the digest system, as well as an annotated system, the initial communication problem between indexer and researcher must be solved. This requires imagination and ingenuity.

5.5.9 Special Cases Digests. Some cases are reported only in special series of reports. Many of these are administrative reports from the many federal administrative agencies. Some of the reports are serviced by their own digest. Others are cited by the looseleaf services. If a case is needed in a peculiar administrative area, look first at the reporter itself and see if a digest accompanies it. Otherwise, look for the looseleaf collection and use the indexer there -- both subject and table of cases. Examples are federal income taxation, U.S. Court of Claims, labor cases, I.C.C. decisions, and F.A.A. reports.

6 THE LAW REPORTS

The fundamental source of law are the constitutions, state and federal. Statutes, administrative rules, and ordinances make up a large body of law. The judicial opinions are the interpreters of the constitutions and statutes. Judicial decisions also are a source of law -- the common law. No law, whether statute or judge-made, is of any force unless it is enforced by a court. The meaning of any law is subject to the opinions of the judges who must enforce that law. The law contained in the reports of the decisions and opinions of the judges is the foundation of the legal system in the common law countries -- Great Britain, United States, Canada, Austrialia, New Zealand, India, Ireland, and the other Commonwealth Nations. The civil law countries -- European Continent, Latin America, and parts of Africa -- are bound to the Roman Code system of law. In that system, judges must look to the statutory codes for the proper interpretation of the statutes. Once an opinion is rendered, it is not later referred to by another judge, as in the common law stare decisis, but the judge looks directly to the code as the source of authority. In the common law countries there is a great deal of law not contained in any statutes -- it is contained in the cumulated judicial opinions from before the year 1200 A.D.

6.1.1 What is a judicial decision and what is a case "report"? There are two primary kinds of judges. One type, called the trial judge, listens to the witnesses, instructs the jury if used, and renders his decision, based upon rules of law applied to the facts that have been found. The "facts" as found by the judge or jury may not necessarily reflect the truth. The other type of judges supervise the work of the trial judges. If an attorney feels that the rule of law applied was inappropriate for the facts, or that the rule of law was incorrectly stated, or that there was a prejudicial error made by the judge in excluding or admitting evidence, including biased jurors, or other rulings during the course of the trial, the attorney may appeal those rulings to a review court. The reviewing court will then have access to the trial transcript, as well as statements of the facts and alleged errors by each attorney in documents called "briefs." The attorneys then appear before the reviewing or appellate court to present oral arguments in behalf of their claims. The court then deliberates and writes an opinion indicating usually: (1) the facts, (2) the disposition in the lower court, (3) the errors alleged to have occurred, (4) a statement of the correct principle of law, including a discussion of the development and reasons for the rules of law involved, with citations to earlier court decisions on the same topic, and (5) the decision in the case with instructions for its disposition.

6.1.2 When appellate courts decide a particular controversy before them, they often write out not only the decision (X wins the lawsuit) but also the facts as they see them and the reasons why they have reached the decision they have made. A simple case might be: A strikes B without B's permission. A has no reason or justification for striking B. B is entitled to recovery of $25 from A for the injury to his person. The decision of the court and the general rule of law announced is that it is unlawful for anyone to strike another person without permission or justification. The court may decide to discuss all of the policy reasons for such a rule, trace the historical treatment of such conduct, examine statutes to see if they are applicable, and discuss cases of a similar nature appearing in other state or federal courts. In fact, most appellate case opinions are complicated discussions of the facts and well-reasoned analysis of

15

previous law and various policy considerations.

6.1.3 Cases are reported by appellate courts. The trial court does not ordinarily prepare a written opinion that is published. A number of the federal district court decisions are reported, but few state court decisions are reported at the trial level. When a case is appealed, however, the reviewing court normally prepares an opinion (in Utah, the Utah Supreme Court; in the federal system, the Circuit Court of Appeals, then the United States Supreme Court; in California, the Court of Appeals, then the California Supreme Court; in New York, the Superior Court, then the Court of Appeals).

6.1.4 The reports of cases in the United States are located in official reports published by the states or the government printing office and in commercially produced reports printed by West Publishing Company. The following chart indicates where the various court opinions are reported.

Abbreviation of Report Citation	Court or State	Name of Official Reporters	West Publishing Company Reporter
U.S. Sup. Ct. U.S. L.ed	United States Supreme Court	U.S. Reports	Supreme Court Reporter U.S. Reports, Lawyer's Edition *
Fed. F.2d	U.S. Circuit Courts of Appeals	none (slip decisions only)	Federal Reporter
F. Supp.	U.S. District Courts	none (slip decisions only)	Federal Supplement
Ala. Ala. App. So.	Alabama	Alabama Reports Alabama Appellate Reports	Southern Reporter

* Lawyers Cooperative Publishing Co./Bancraft-Whitney Publishing Co.

Alaska P. P.2d	Alaska	Alaska Reports (terminated with v. 17)	Pacific Reporter
Ariz. P. P.2d	Arizona	Arizona Reports	Pacific Reporter
Ark. S.W. S.W.2d	Arkansas	Arkansas Reports	South Western Reporter
Cal. Cal. App. Cal. Rptr. P. P.2d	California	California Reports California Appellate Reports	Pacific Reporter California Reporter
Colo. P. P.2d	Colorado	Colorado Reports Colorado Appellate Reports	Pacific Reporter
Conn. A. A.2d	Connecticut	Connecticut Reports	Atlantic Reporter
Del. Del. Ch. A. A.2d	Delaware	Delaware Reports Delaware Chancery Reports	Atlantic Reporter
A.2d F. Supp.	District of Columbia	none	Atlantic Reporter Federal Supplement
Fla. So.	Florida	Florida Reports (terminated with v. 160)	Southern Reporter
Ga. S.E. S.E.2d	Georgia	Georgia Reports	South Eastern Reporter
Hawaii P. P.2d	Hawaii	Hawaii Reports	Pacific Reporter

17

Idaho P. P.2d	Idaho	Idaho Reports	Pacific Reporter
Ill., Ill. App., N.E. N.E.2d	Illinois	Illinois Reports Illinois Appellate Reports	North Eastern Reporter
Ind., Ind. App., N.E. N.E.2d	Indiana	Indiana Reports Indiana Appellate Reports	North Eastern Reporter
Iowa N.W. N.W.2d	Iowa	Iowa Reports	North Western Reporter
Kan., Kan App., P. P.2d	Kansas	Kansas Reports Kansas Appellate Reports	Pacific Reporter
Ky., Ky. L. Rptr. Ky. Dec. S.W. S.W.2d	Kentucky	Kentucky Reports (terminated with v. 314) Kentucky Law Reporter Kentucky Decisions	South Western Reporter
La., La. Ann. La. App. So.	Louisiana	Louisiana Reports Louisiana Annotated Reports Louisiana Appellate Reports	Southern Reporter
Me. A. A.2d	Maine	Maine Reports	Atlantic Reporter

Md. A. A.2d	Maryland	Maryland Reports	Atlantic Reporter
Mass. N.E. N.E.2d	Massachu- setts	Massachu- setts Re- ports	North East- ern Repor- ter
Mich. N.W. N.W.2d	Michigan	Michigan Reports	North West- ern Repor- ter
Minn. N.W. N.W.2d	Minnesota	Minnesota Reports	North West- ern Repor- ter
Miss. So.	Mississippi	Mississippi Reports	Southern Reporter
Mo., Mo. App., S.W. S.W.2d	Missouri	Missouri Re- ports (termi- nated with v. 365) Miss- ouri Appel- late Reports (terminated with v. 241)	South West- ern Repor- ter
Mont. P. P.2d	Montana	Montana Reports	Pacific Reporter
Neb. N.W. N.W.2d	Nebraska	Nebraska Reports	North West- ern Repor- ter
Nev. P. P.2d	Nevada	Nevada Reports	Pacific Reporter
N.H. A. A.2d	New Hamp- shire	New Hamp- shire Re- ports	Atlantic Reporter

19

N.J. N.J. Eq. A. A.2d	New Jersey	New Jersey Law Reports New Jersey Equity Reports	Atlantic Reporter
N.M. P. P.2d	New Mexico	New Mexico Reports	Pacific Reporter
N.Y. N.Y. App. N.Y. Supp. N.E. N.E.2d	New York	New York Reports New York Appellate Reports	North Eastern Reporter
N.C. S.E. S.E.2d	North Carolina	North Carolina Reports	South Eastern Reporter
N.D. N.W. N.W.2d	North Dakota	North Dakota Reports (terminated with v. 79)	North Western Reporter
Ohio, Ohio App., N.E. N.E.2d	Ohio	Ohio Reports Ohio Appellate Reports	North Eastern Reporter
Okla. P. P.2d	Oklahoma	Oklahoma Reports (terminated with v. 208)	Pacific Reporter
Pa., Pa. Super., Pa. D.C. A. A.2d	Pennsylvania	Pennsylvania State Reports Pennsylvania Superior Reports Pennsylvania District & County Reports	Atlantic Reporter

R.I. A.A.2d	Rhode Island	Rhode Island Reports	Atlantic Reporter
S.C. S.E. S.E.2d	South Carolina	South Caro- lina Reports	South East- ern Repor- ter
S.D. N.W. N.W.2d	South Dakota	South Dako- ta Reports	North West- ern Repor- ter
Tenn. Tenn. App. S.W. S.W.2d	Tennessee	Tennessee Reports Tennessee Appellate Reports	South West- ern Repor- ter
Tex. Tex. App. Tex. Crim. S.W. S.W.2d	Texas	Texas Re- ports (ter- minated with v. 163) Texas Ap- pellate Re- ports Texas Criminal Re- ports (ter- minated with v. 172)	South West- ern Repor- ter
Utah Utah 2d P. P.2d	Utah	Utah Reports 1st Series Utah Reports 2d Series	Pacific Re- porter
Vt. A. A.2d	Vermont	Vermont Re- ports	Atlantic Reporter
Va. S.E. S.E.2d	Virginia	Virginia Reports	South East- ern Repor- ter
Wash. P. P.2d	Washington	Washington Reports	Pacific Reporter

W. Va. S.E. S.E.2d	West Virginia	West Virginia Reports	South Eastern Reporter
Wis. N.W. N.W.2d	Wisconsin	Wisconsin Reports	North Western Reporter
Wyo. P. P.2d	Wyoming	Wyoming Reports (terminated with v. 80)	Pacific Reporter

6.1.5 Citations. Lawyers have invented a shorthand technique to describe where a case report is printed. The citation also contains the date of final decision as well as valuable subsequent case history. A typical citation may appear as follows: Shelly Oil Co. v. FPC, 375 F.2d 6 (10th Cir. 1967) modified on other grounds, 390 U.S. 747, 88 S.Ct. 1344, 20 L.Ed.2d 312 (1968). This tells us that Shelly Oil Company was suing the Federal Power Commission in federal court. It was appealed to the 10th Circuit Court of Appeals (Utah is in the 10th Judicial Circuit). The opinion delivered by the 10th Circuit is found in Volume 375 of the West Publishing Company's Federal Reporter, Second Series at page 6. The case was decided in 1967. The case was then appealed to the United States Supreme Court where it was modified -- but not on the proposition for which the case is being cited for as authority. The decision for the Supreme Court may be found in Volume 390 of the United States Reports (the official reporter) at page 747; in Volume 88 of the Supreme Court Reporter (West version) at page 1344; in Volume 20 of the United States Reports Lawyer's Edition, Second Series (ALR version) at page 312. The case was decided in 1968. The citation does not tell what the issue in the case was, or the holding, or the facts -- it merely is a shorthand method of telling a lawyer where to find the report of that case. If the citation is available, one needs merely to locate the set of reports and select the correct volume and page. See the Harvard White Book for correct citation forms for state courts. The normal citation is: Farnsworth v. Peshell, 22 U.2d 311, 314, 498 P.2d 30, 33 (1971).

6.2 The Federal Reports. The United States judiciary are divided into two groups (state and federal) consonant with the constitutional design of federalism. Each group has important jurisdiction and so mentioning the federal system first is not an attempt to downplay the vital and final role played by the state courts.

6.2.1 Jurisdiction of Federal Courts. The U.S. Constitution, art. III, sec. 1 vests the judicial power of the United States "in one supreme court, and in such inferior courts as the Congress may from time to time ordain and establish." The Congress has since then created eleven judicial circuit courts of appeals to hear appeals from the numerous federal trial or district courts. In addition, two administrative appeals courts, the Court of Claims and the Court of Customs and Patent Appeals, are given status similar to that enjoyed by the courts of appeals. Sec. 2 states the jurisdiction of the federal courts as follows: "all cases, in law and equity, arising under this constitution, the laws of the United States, and treaties made, or which shall be made, under their authority; to all cases affecting ambassadors, other public ministers and consuls; to all cases of admiralty and maritime jurisdictions; to controversies to which the United States shall be a party; to controversies between two or more states, between a state and citizens of another state, between citizens of different states, between citizens of the same state claiming lands under grants of different states, and between a state, or the citizens thereof, and foreign States, citizens or subjects." This means, in most cases, that in order to invoke federal jurisdictions, the case must present a "federal question" or must involve "diversity of citizenship." In addition, there must be an amount in controversy over $10,000 (the amount is set by federal statute). In some cases, Congress has vested the federal courts with original jurisdiction in such matters as antitrust violations.

6.2.2 The Supreme Court has special jurisdiction over certain cases. These cases must be brought only to the Supreme Court. Art. III, sec. 2 states: "In all cases affecting ambassadors, other public ministers and consuls, and those in which a state shall be party, the Supreme court shall have original jurisdiction." Its other caseload is appellate. The Congress has allowed the Supreme Court to choose its own caseload, with several exceptions, chief of which are where a state court has declared a federal law unconstitutional, or where a federal court has declared a state law unconstitutional. All other cases may come to the Supreme Court only if that court issues a writ of certiorari (review). If four justices or more cannot agree to hear a case for which a petition for a writ of certiorari has been filed, the petition is denied. The Constitution's provision

23

for appellate review is as follows: "In all the other cases before mentioned, the supreme court shall have appellate jurisdiction, both as to law and fact, with such exceptions, and under such regulations as the Congress shall make." (Art. III, sec. 2).

6.2.3 Reports of Supreme Court Decisions. Full written opinions of the U.S. Supreme Court are printed in "slip decision" form -- e.g., individually by the Government Printing Office (G.P.O.). Monday is opinion day for the Court. These slip opinions are released to the press, and mailed to all government document depository libraries and to all who subscribe to the slip decisions through the G.P.O. Time of delivery varies, but usually is a week, or more, later because of delays of mailing. Important decisions are reported in the New York Times as well as many local newspapers via the UPI and AP wire services. The Bureau of National Affairs (BNA) prints full opinions in its weekly service, U.S. Law Week, Supreme Court section, which arrives by air mail at many libraries. Commerce Clearing House (CCH) also has a weekly Supreme Court reporting service. Upon request, either will air mail their services, which speeds access. The BNA Law Week series is the easiest method to use to find current cases.

6.2.4 "Advance sheets" are published by the G.P.O. as well as by two commercial law reporters. The official edition, a brown paperback, United States Reports, is printed periodically when sufficient reports are written to publish an issue. It is subject to revision. The Supreme Court Reporter (West Publishing Company) also provides an advance sheet copy with the West digesting key number system of indexing in each issue, with cumulative indexing through later issues until the bound volume is printed. The United States Supreme Court Reports Lawyer's Edition (Bancroft-Whitney Publishing Company) is in advance sheet form also, and is indexed through its own digest. The easiest to use in searching for needed cases is the Supreme Court Reporter -- although this is strictly a matter of personal preference. Each reporter indexes all cases reported or dealt with by appellant and by respondent names.

6.2.5 The bound permanent volumes of the United States Reports contain all full opinions. The Supreme Court Reporter and the Lawyer's Edition also contain the full opinions. Between the three reporters, almost all of the memorandum decisions, per curiam decisions, denials of writs of certiorari, noting probable jurisdiction, amicus curiae briefs, etc., are printed. The Journal of the U.S. Supreme Court or U.S. Law Week should be consulted to insure a full history of action on a case before the Supreme Court. Law Week is easier to use.

6.2.6 Citation to the various early Supreme Court reporters is misleading because of historical reasons. The first ninety volumes of the United States Reports (citation: U.S.) were reported by various entrepreneurs whose names appear on the reports. Thus, the following table indicates the proper citation and name of the first ninety volumes (note the necessary parenthetical reference to the names of the early reporters):

1 U.S. (1 Dall.) - (1790-	Dallas
4 U.S. (4 Dall.) - -1800)	
5 U.S. (1 Cranch) - (1801-	Cranch
13 U.S. (9 Cranch) - -1815)	
14 U.S. (1 Wheat.) - (1816-	Wheaton
25 U.S. (12 Wheat.) - -1827)	
26 U.S. (1 Pet.) - (1816-	Peters
41 U.S. (16 Pet.) - -1842)	
42 U.S. (1 How.) - (1843-	Howard
65 U.S. (24 How.) - -1860)	
66 U.S. (1 Black) - (1861-	Black
67 U.S. (2 Black) - -1862)	
68 U.S. (1 Wall.) - (1863-	Wallace
90 U.S. (23 Wall.) - -1874)	

Lawyers Edition covers from volume 1 up to the current time, but renumbered its volumes (2d series) with volume 352 U.S. Reports. Since it includes several official volumes in each of its volumes, with a digest, index, and annotations of important cases, its citations are not the same as the official volume and page number. Thus 383 U.S. 413 (volume 383 of the official U.S. Reports report appearing on page 413) become 16 L.Ed 2d 1 (volume 16, Lawyers Edition, second series, at page 1). The Supreme Court Reporter does not begin until volume 106 of the official edition and once again, the citation and paging are not the same. 383 U.S. 413 (1966) becomes 86 S. Ct. 975 (1966). There are tables in each bound volume showing how to transfer a citation to the other editions. The same information is in the Blue Book of the National Reporter System Digest (American Digest System), as well as in the U.S. Reports Shepard's Citations volume. Notations in the two unofficial editions indicate precisely where each official page begins.

6.2.7 Other Federal Decisions. The Federal Reporter covers all written opinions of the (Circuit) Courts of Appeals, as well as the decisions in the Court of Claims and the Court of Customs and Patent Appeals. Each appellate court releases slip decisions, which are located in various libraries -- usually within the circuits. U.S. Law Week picks up the important federal courts of appeals decisions and reports a short synopsis in the General Law section. The Federal Reporter advance sheets precede the regular bound volumes. Federal Cases picks up from 1880 back to 1789. It was printed in the 1890's and is a compilation of earlier decisions. The arrangement is alphabetical by case name and includes an arbitrary number from 1 to 18,313. The earlier Federal Reporters also contained reports of selected opinions from the federal district courts. The Federal Supplement, begun in 1932, picks up the district court opinions. Not all federal district court opinions are printed -- it is discretionary with the trial judge. U.S. Law Week General Law section covers the most notable cases (notable to the editor of Law Week). The Federal Supplement advance sheets precede the bound volume by several weeks.

6.2.8 Federal administrative courts and tribunals publish official reports. Most of the significant cases are reported in C.C.H., Prentice-Hall, or B.N.A. looseleaf services, which index as well as print reports and also include editorial comments that are very useful.

6.3 State Reports. The West National Reporter System covers all state supreme court decisions as well as the lower appellate decisions of New York and California in their own series. Not every state publishes a separate "official" reporter. See page 18 of the Harvard White Book for the termination dates for Alaska, Florida, Kentucky, Missouri, North Dakota, Oklahoma, Texas and Wyoming. These states rely on the West National Reporter System exclusively.

6.3.1 Proper citation form for published legal writing requires both the official citation and the parallel citation to the unofficial reports, except for U.S. Supreme Court decisions, e.g., 110 U. 311, 398 P.2d 610 (1963). Each unofficial Supreme Court reporter is careful to print official page and volume numbers in the text of reports, so it is not necessary to give the full parallel citation, although many non-law review publications elect to include all three citations for Supreme Court cases. See White Book, pp. 1-15.

7 UPDATING CASE LAW

Just as Congress and state legislatures amend their laws

from time to time, courts often change judicial rules of law. In the case of statutes, the legislating body repeals the former law and rewrites it to conform to the amendments. Courts do not always indicate that a previously announced or affirmed rule of law is overruled or discredited. In fact the court opinion may not even mention the existence of a prior opinion. When a seemingly relevant case is found, that case must be verified as still being valid law. This procedure of searching for conflicting decisions has been minimized by the publication of Shepard's Citations. The effort of the Shepard's editors is to indicate after each case citation whether the case has ever been cited in another case, and if so, whether the later citing overrules, follows, distinguishes, etc., the earlier case. The Shepard's books are arranged according to the names of the reporter -- e.g., all Federal Reporter citations are in the Federal Reporter Shepard's Citator. If the overruling court is dishonest about its acts and fails to cite the overruled case, Shepard's will not reflect the change, so the digest topic and key number for the earlier case must be searched and updated for conflicting judicial doctrines from the same or a higher court. Both procedures must be followed to avoid embarrassing error and subsequent folly.

8 THE VALUE OF JUDICIAL PRECEDENT AND DICTUM

8.1 What weight does a court opinion carry? The answer to this question depends upon many factors. The first question must be what is the age of the case, when was it decided? Decisions may be worth more because of old age, but also may be worth very little. Marbury v. Madison, 5 U.S. (1 Cranch) 137 (1803), is an example of a case gaining value as it grows older. But the decisions of the Superior Court of New York State in 1830 on the validity of an arrest procedure may be meaningless. The date of a case must be carefully noted. Generally, the older it is, the less reliable it is. The next question: which court decided the case? The reports of the Supreme Court of the United States carry considerably more weight in the federal district courts of Texas than do federal district court opinions in New Hampshire. A lower court is always bound by a higher court in the same system. Thus, all trial courts in California are bound by the decisions of the California Supreme Court. If a California trial court were to substitute its own rule for that of the California Supreme Court, the aggrieved party could appeal the "error" and the trial court's decision would be overturned by the higher court. The California Supreme Court must follow the U.S. Supreme Court decisions only if a matter of federal constitutional law is involved. It may choose to follow the decisions of the U.S. Supreme Court in other than constitutional law cases. It may also choose to follow other state court decisions, but it need not unless a principle in the law of conflicts of law is involved, and then it is only out of comity towards the other states.

8.2 The opinion in a case contains at least one rule of law -- the holding of the court based upon the particular facts. The language used by the court in articulating policy reasons for the decision, policy considerations, previous decisions, the effect of particular statutes, and the rationale governing the holding of the court on the set of facts before it is called dictum. The holding of the court is normally quite a narrow principle of law used as a basis for ruling upon a unique set of facts. This rule of law becomes legal precedent and binding on lower courts and applies to similar fact situations in the future unless later reversed. On the other hand, dictum only has a persuasive value. The arguments expressed in support of a ruling indicate the attitude of a court towards the legal interest involved. The dictum may be used in support of later court holdings applying the same rule of law to different kinds of fact situations having the same general characteristics as the original fact situation. For example: A sustains an injury caused by the wrongful actions of B who willfully strikes A with his fist. The strict holding of the court might be: "A may recover damages from B for intentionally and wrongfully striking A." The court may then discuss the reasons for allowing recovery: "When one acts carelessly or intentionally causes another harm, then the actor should compensate the party thus harmed." Note that the holding is limited to specific facts involving intentional conduct. The dictum enlarges the specific facts to a principle. In a later case, C negligently tries to hit a ball and strikes D. The court may then say, "Relying on the case of A v. B, C must compensate D for C's careless act." Technically, the court has made an error. The case of A v. B only stands for the proposition that one must pay for damages caused by intentional acts, not for careless or negligent acts. What the later court has relied upon is not a holding in law, but mere dictum. Nevertheless, the courts often will do this -- it involes cutting through the traditional rules of law to determine the rationale for the rule.

Chapter 3

USING THE STATUTES

9 CONSTITUTIONS

(1) Federal Constitution

9.1 The U.S. Constitution is the supreme law of the land. It represents a grant of power from the people to the federal government. Unless the people amend (change) the Constitution, no laws, treaties or other acts of government are valid unless enacted pursuant to a provision of the Constitution. The words of the Constitution must be interpreted, however, and meaning attached to the individual provisions. Early in the history of the United States, the Supreme Court decided it was the final interpreter of the Constitution by implication. The other federal powers -- Congress and the president -- acquiesced in that decision. The Supreme Court, then, may state whether or not any act of government is repugnant to the limited grant of power conferred to that government by the people.

9.2 The Constitution itself provides the starting point for anyone doing research in "constitutional law." It is published in the front of each state code as well as in the front of each of the United States Code compilations: United States Code, United States Code Annotated, and Federal Code Service.

9.3 The Constitution is divided into seven articles with twenty-five additional articles, or amendments, and begins with a short preamble. The preamble to the Constitution has taken on nearly a separate meaning since it provides a background or purpose statement for the individual articles. The statements: "insure domestic tranquility, provide for the common defense, promote the general welfare" seem to have nearly separate importance. Article I establishes and defines the Congress and its powers. The tenth amendment further delimits the authority of Congress by stating that all powers not delegated to the United States or prohibited to the states are reserved to the states or the people. Among the important provisions in Article I are those of sec. 8: the power to tax, to borrow money, to regulate commerce, to declare war, and to raise and maintain an army and navy. Article II regulates the office of the President. Article III creates and regulates the federal judiciary. Article IV governs state relations. Article V provides for amendments. Article VI contains the supremacy clause. Article VIII provides for ratification. The Bill of Rights is contained in the first ten amendments. The other significant amendment is the fourteenth amendment, which is used to funnel the Bill of Rights into a prohibition to the states via the due process and equal protection clauses of the fourteenth amendment.

9.4 The provisions to the Constitution are indexed by individual words in each of the three federal codes. For example, on page LV of the United States Code is the "Analytical Index to the Constitution of the United States and the Amendments thereto."

9.5 The Constitution is a very complex document because the language is so broad. The current meaning of the Constitution lies not in the language of the document itself, but in the interpretation by the courts. The Supreme Court is the final authority on the meaning of the Constitution. However, it often declines review of lower federal court decisions and state supreme court decisions interpreting constitutional provisions. And, unless the party complaining of a deprivation of a constitutional right pursues his claim through the appellate courts, as a practical matter the trial court determines what the meaning of the Constitution is.

9.6 The primary search method for constitutional doctrines is through the index and case notes to U.S. Code Annotated and the court report digests. The most useful of the digests is the Modern Federal Practice Digest and its earlier edition, Federal Digest. These sets contain citations and synopses of all reported federal court opinions, which include the U.S. Supreme Court, the Courts of Appeals, and the basic trial courts, the federal district courts. The basic arrangement of case law is by traditional legal subjects. The best entrance tool is the Descriptive Word Index volumes, which converts layman's language as well as specific problem descriptions into the index/subject law language. For example, a problem involving dismissal of male students from high school for wearing long hair in violation of a dress and grooming code would be located as follows: turning first to the two volume Descriptive Word Index Cumulative Supplement of the Modern Federal Practice Digest, a search could be made under any of the following specific topics: "Schools and School Districts," "Long Hair," "Long Haired Male Students,"

"Dress Code," "Hair," and "Pupils." Two general topics could also be used: "Due Process of Law," and "Equal Protection of Laws." Under each heading is a short description of the subject such as this one located under the heading "Schools and School Dist.": "Long hair worn by boys, regulations banning. Schools 172." In the main volumes under the general topic "schools," beginning at key number 172 and continuing, are the short statements of law dealing with this subject as well as case citations.

9.7 Two smaller digests contain only U.S. Supreme Court cases: the United States Supreme Court Digest, which is keyed to the West digest and reporting system, and the U.S. Supreme Court Digest Annotated, which is used with the Lawyer's Edition version of the United States Reports (tied with A.L.R.). The value of these two sets is that both are complete without using any other set except their own pocket supplements. The weakness of each is the lack of digested notes to the lower federal courts or to any state cases.

9.8 The annotated versions of the U.S. Code, the United States Code Annotated and the United States Code Service, contain a very helpful system of annotating particular articles and amendments. This service is very useful for some clauses, but not so valuable for others. The index volumes contain access by specific subject but the Modern Federal Practice Digest Descriptive Word Index volumes are more helpful. As may be expected, there are many hundreds of cases construing such constitutional clauses as the commerce clause, the due process clause, and the freedom of press clause. These must be approached with special care since particular problems must be researched specifically and cautiously to avoid error.

9.9 The intent of the Constitution's original framers is difficult to research, but not impossible. No formal minutes of the debates or considerations leading to the compromise positions were taken. The notes taken by James Madison are quite extensive, however, and appear in two volumes, The Papers of James Madison. The notion of federal supremacy is covered well in The Federalist, by Hamilton, Madison, and Jay. Other sources are also available. Treatises on the Constitution are available, including a number of legal casebooks used in law school constitutional law courses.

9.10 There are other methods for researching constitutional law problems, but they involve the standard techniques for locating appropriate case law, such as use of the American

Digest System, American Law Reports, encyclopedias, treatises, Index to Legal Periodicals, etc., as described elsewhere in this book.

(2) State Constitutions

9.11 State constitutions are located in the front of each state code, e.g., Volume 1 of Arizona Statutes Annotated, and Utah Code Annotated. Cite section 7, article 4, of the New Mexico state constitution as follows: N.M.Const. art. 4, § 7. Each constitution is indexed in the general index volume. Caution: do not rely solely on a pamphlet copy of a state constitution since pamphlets do not contain court opinions determing the meaning of the constitutional provisions. The constitution appearing in the compiled laws for each state is annotated with court decisions as well as its history. For many of the states it is necessary or desirable to get some further historical background of a constitutional provision. Many states have published the proceedings in their constitutional conventions. Another source is local law review articles or bar journal articles. A looseleaf service that updates constitutions is U.S. Constitutions: National and State, combined with Index Digest to State Constitutions, published by Oceana Publications, Inc.

10 FEDERAL STATUTES

10.1 Introduction to Basic Research. The current in-force laws of the United States (federal laws) are compiled by subject in the United States Code, 1970 edition with annual supplements, cited: U.S.C. (1970). This is the "official" edition printed by the Government Printing Office. Certain parts of the United States Code are not "positive law," e.g., Congress has not enacted some titles appearing in the United States Code as the final language. From time to time the printer fails to transfer the language Congress wrote as the final bill into the Code. Thus the original source should be consulted for the following titles of United States Code in the Statutes at Large: Titles 2, 7, 8, 11, 12, 15, 16, 19, 20, 21, 22, 24, 25, 26, 27, 29, 30, 31, 33, 36, 40, 41, 42, 43, 45, 46, 47, 48, 49, and 50. The 1970 codification is supplemented by bound annual volumes. The only supplements published to date are the 1971 and 1972 supplements. Thus it is apparent that a more current codification of federal law should be used. The best is the United States Code

Annotated (U.S.C.A.). When using U.S.C.A. (or any rapidly changing set of law books) it is imperative that all supplements -- pocket supplements in the back of each volume, bound single volume cumulative supplements shelved at the end of the set, and paper supplements shelved next to the bound supplements -- be consulted. See ¶ 10.4.4 infra, for a discussion of U.S.C.A.

10.2 Enactment of Federal Law. The most basic federal "laws" are bills enacted by each house of the Congress and then signed by the President into "law." The "Laws of the United States" when enacted within the scope of the Constitution become the law of the land and binding on everyone, including the states. Other sources of federal law include executive orders of the President, treaties of the United States, rules and orders of the federal administrative agencies (such as the S.E.C., F.A.A., F.C.C., and I.C.C.), orders of the cabinet officers, orders of the military officers, and Congressional resolutions.

10.3 Legislative History. Each member of Congress may "introduce" bills and resolutions into consideration by the house in which he serves. Citation: unenacted bills -- Senate: S. 116, 91st Cong., 1st Sess. §§ 2-4 (1972); House: H. 21, 91st Cong. 1st Sess. § 2 (1972). See Rule 5, Whitebook. The bill is introduced, assigned a number, printed separately, and sent to the appropriate committee. The unenacted bill is referred to as a "slip bill" in the library. Hundreds of bills are printed each year. They are filed by number. If a bill is reintroduced it is assigned a new number. Status, number, name of bill, or sponsor can be located most quickly in CCH Congressional Index, which is updated weekly. The bill is then considered by the committee and the committee's subcommittees as appropriate. If the bill is of some importance, the committee may decide to hold public hearings. Those hearings are printed verbatim unless libel or national security prohibits transcripts of the entire hearing. The discussions in the hearing reports are important sources of "legislative history." The meaning of a law may be obscured by faulty language so courts may sometimes rely upon the Congressional hearings to ascertain the proper intent of Congress and thus the meaning of the law. "Hearing Reports" are located in the government documents collection of most libraries although some libraries will catalog them as regular books. They may be traced through the main card catalog, the documents card catalog, or the Monthly Catalog. The hearings that are printed are indexed in several places: "History of Bills Enacted Into Public Law" appearing in the Daily Digest of the Congressional Record;

CCH Congressional Index; The Congressional Monitor; Cumulative Index of Congressional Committee Hearings; United States Code Congressional and Administrative News (used with U.S. Code Annotated); and Congressional Information Service. Hearings are difficult to use at best. They are not indexed individually although a table of contents usually indicates the order of witnesses. Unless a detailed or obscure point is sought, an easier source of information, if available, is the committee report. Often, however, the report is not detailed or specific enough to be helpful as a source of legislative intent for individual sections of a particular bill. Discussion of the bill on the floor of the house is reported in the Congressional Record. The explaination of the bill in the debates appearing in the Congressional Record are very often cited in court opinions as evidencing the proper meaning of a disputed section of law. If both houses pass similar bills, a joint conference committee meets to iron out provisions making the bill acceptable to both houses. The conference committe report contains the summary of this committee work.

A bill becomes law after passage in both houses of Congress and approval by the President (or enactment over the President's veto). Laws are categorized as public or private and are numbered sequentially during the two-year Congressional term. New laws are available in several forms: slip laws individually printed; U.S. Code Congressional and Administrative News Service accompanying U.S. Code Annotated is the easiest source to find and use; the new laws service in the U.S. Code Service; and new laws with special merit appear in U.S. Law Week -- General Section. The G.P.O. prints Statutes at Large, an official publication with all laws in chronological order as enacted. Amendments to previous laws are in chronological order also and are reconciled only in the various editions of the U.S. Code. There are various tables in the Codes and Statutes at Large tracing and cross referencing the various laws. A popular name table is also in each set as well as in Shepard's to locate laws, such as the "Taft-Hartley Act."

10.4 Researching in Federal Statutes. Statutory research requires precision and must be exhaustive. There are three methods for finding relevant statutory provisions and the meanings of those provisions.

10.4.1 Popular Name. If the act is known by a popular name such as the Wagner Act, the Uniform Time Act of 1966, or the Taft-Hartley Act, then the statute can be located in the U.S. Code and the Statutes at Large through the popular name tables in the index to the Code, and individually in the Statutes at Large. Once located, there is the simple matter of finding the right provision. In the several editions of the Code each major area is preceded by an index.

10.4.2 Subject. The Codes are indexed by subject. The Statutes at Large are not. Some ingenuity must be used in finding the proper subject as indexed.

10.4.3 Citation. The Codes are cited as follows: official name or popular name; title; U.S.C., U.S.C.A., or U.S.C.S. (formerly F.C.A.); sections; and date of compilation. U.S.C. is the official edition and is preferred. See White Book, rule 4:1. A typical citation is Declaratory Judgment Act, 28 U.S.C.§§ 2201-02 (1970). The Statutes at Large are cited when the law is scattered in the code, not in force, or is used in historical connotation: Federal Corrupt Practice Act of 1925, ch. 368, tit. III, 43 Stat. 1070 (codified in scattered sections of 2, 18 U.S.C.). Statutory citations are picked up in treatises, cases, law review articles, briefs, indexes, other statutes, etc.

10.4.4 Analysis. The location of a single provision of a statute by itself does not end your research. The particular section may have been declared unconstitutional by a court. The section may have been the subject of significant litigation and may have been "changed" by court or administrative modification of the statute's meaning. The section may have been repealed, amended, or revised by later legislation. Thus, considerable additional mechanical checking must be done as well as analysis of the history of the law, both before and after enactment. All of the annotations in U.S.C,A or U.S.C.S. must be carefully scrutinized and questionable annotations should be checked further by reading the actual case. The facts must be carefully compared to the conduct affected by the statute and other sections checked to insure that the selected section is the only one that applies. Often a good law review article or treatise will discuss much of the historical and judicial actions affecting a statute, thus saving a great deal of time, as well as identifying collateral statutes of importance.

In addition to the case law annotations and history cited in U.S.C.A. or U.S.C.S., it is important to check for administrative rules promulgated by administrative agencies as authorized by statute. For example, the Internal Revenue Code, while extremely specific in many of its provisions, is supplemented by hundreds of very specific regulations. Administrative regulations appear first in the Federal Register and then in the Code of Federal Regulations (C.F.R.). The most complex administrative and statutory enactments are reported in looseleaf services updated weekly.

10.5 Treaties. Another source of federal law are treaties negotiated and signed by the President and ratified by a two-third's majority of the Senate. Treaties appear in Treaties and Other International Agreements (T.I.A.S.). Prior to 1950, treaties were printed in Statutes at Large.

11 STATE STATUTES

11.1 State laws are contained in several places -- the session laws, state code or compiled laws, administrative regulations, county and municipal ordinances, and special district regulations. The most important research tool for state law is the compiled statutes or codes. The individual state code, such as the California Code, contains a detailed index by subject. As with all law indexes, ingenuity must be used to find particular subjects. For example, in looking for a criminal statute defining child-stealing, the words "children," "infants," "juveniles," "wards," "stealing," "abducting," "kidnapping," or other related topics might be used as the indexing word. Each code has the state constitution with annotations. Annotations are short statements of court decisions affecting a particular provision or section. The current text of state general laws is provided with historical notes (date the law was enacted, subsequent amendments), cross references to similar laws in other states, and case law annotations. The latest information is located in pocket supplements or bound individual supplements. These absolutely must be carefully checked to bring the material up to date. In addition to the general state laws, the codes also contain rules of court and rules of civil procedure, along with various sample practice forms. State codes do not contain county, city, and local governmental unit ordinances, or state administrative regulations.

11.2 Municipal and administrative regulations of all types are not widely distributed and are often difficult to locate for smaller areas. Special purpose districts often do not publish their rules. Large state administrative agencies, such as tax collecting agencies, will publish explanatory regulations, which are often also published commercially by such companies as C.C.H., Prentice-Hall, B.N.A., etc. Since local ordinances are frequently difficult to locate and update, it is wise to contact the secretary of the local government authority to see if any new changes have been made to existing regulations.

11.3 State and local laws are also listed in various comparative commentaries. The Martindale-Hubbell Law Directory publishes a digest of the major statutes and common law in Volume V. West publishes a set digesting the Uniform Acts. Shepard's prints a very useful digest of municipal ordinances. Shepard's also provides citations for ordinances and state statutes.

12 ADMINISTRATIVE REGULATIONS

12.1 Administrative agencies in the federal government constitute a "fourth branch." They are given broad powers of rule-making and adjudication subject to review by federal courts and by Congress. Their legislative and judicial functions are supposed to be exercised within clearly defined legislative grants of power, but in fact they operate largely unsupervised and in broad general areas. The function of the administrative agency is to act in a discretionary area -- applying specific rules to concrete individual circumstances, which is impossible for Congress or the courts to do. The lack, however, of standards, published reasons, findings of fact, rules, review, and guidelines often leads them to act capriciously and in an atmosphere where they are unchecked, unstructured, and unconfined. This atmosphere presents a climate where there is a great lack of justice to the individual.

The Administrative Procedure Act of 1946 was amended by the Freedom of Information Act, revising 5 U.S.C. § 552 et al (1970), and there seems to be a general move to clarify the unchecked discretion administrative agencies have been working in. See 1970 Supplement to Administrative Law Treatise. Kenneth C. Davis.

12.2 The types of actions performed by administrative agencies are not at all limited. They make rules, find facts and promulgate orders based upon decisions; they write no-action letters, render advisory opinions, prosecute, and hold hearings. They also review decisions made internally, and recommend new legislation.

12.3 The sudden rise in administrative agencies and their complex activities resulted in confusion about the status of administrative rules and regulations. The Congress enacted the

Federal Register Act in 1936, which provided for publication in the Federal Register of any administrative rule or regulation having any general applicability and having a general legal effect, such as imposing obligations or penalties, or granting rights. It is several hundred volumes in length and is published daily. It is indexed by individual volume. The Federal Register in not extremely useful in finding the current status of regulations. For this purpose, consult the Code of Federal Regulations (C.F.R.).

12.4 The Code of Federal Regulations (C.F.R.) codified federal administrative rules and regulations. It is reprinted each year and contains regulations in force as of January 1 of each year. The regulations are arranged by fifty titles, similar to the arrangement of the U.S. Code. For example, the federal Internal Revenue Code is located in Title 26 of the U.S. Code; regulations issued by the Commissioner of Internal Revenue and/or the Secretary of the Treasury (Treasury Decision) are codified in Title 26 of the Code of Federal Regulations. A discussion of the meaning of the term "adjusted gross income" is located in the Internal Revenue Code at section 62, title 26. Similarly, a discussion of the regulations of the Internal Revenue Service (IRS) is located in title 26 C.F.R. at section 62. Both citations would be: 26 U.S.C. § 62 (1970); 26 C.F.R. 1.62-1 (1973).

Regulations become law first by being issued in proposed form and published in the Federal Register. Interested members of the public are invited to comment on the proposed regulation. The issuing agency must wait at least thirty days for comments from the public. Then the issuing agency revises the proposed regulation and the final version of the regulation is publised in the Federal Register, which is prima facie evidence of the text of the original documents. Then, each year, the final regulations are merged into the Code of Federal Regulations and the new codification is published.

C.F.R. is indexed by a separate index volume, and the indexing words are descriptive and topical. As with all law, C.F.R. is always being amended by final regulations published in the Federal Register. New regulations in the Federal Register affecting any part of the C.F.R. are indicated in a table called the Codification Guide, which is included in each daily edition of the Register and is cumulated monthly and quarterly.

In addition to the regulations and rules of federal administrative agencies published in the Federal Register and

C.F.R., executive orders of the President are published in the Federal Register. Decisions of the administrative agencies are not published in either the Federal Register or C.F.R., but are published separately, and may be located in any general federal depository library or law library.

13 ADMINISTRATIVE DECISIONS

The decisions of the federal administrative agencies are generally reported in separate bound volumes published by the Government Printing Office. For example, beginning in 1934, the National Labor Relations Board printed its decisions and orders in volume 1 et seq. of the N.L.R.A. Decisions and Orders. While each of the N.L.R.B. volumes is individually indexed, there is no general subject or case index to this set of books now containing over three hundred volumes. In nearly every major area of administrative law, a private publishing company has prepared a subject-oriented treatment of that area, including an index to the official government administrative agency reports, along with a table of cases indicating the citation and location of each of the cases reported. Many of these treatises on administrative law are looseleaf and are supplemented as often as weekly. For example, Commerce Clearing House (CCH) Labor Law Reporter contains the index for the N.L.R.A. Decisions and Orders, along with a definitive discussion of the statutory law, regulations, court decisions, and administrative agency decisions. The same coverage is also given to labor law through the Bureau of National Affairs (BNA) Labor Relations Report, as well as other similar reporting services.

14 RULES OF COURT

All judicial systems provide rules governing the conduct of litigation in those systems. The U.S. Supreme Court promulgates general rules of procedure for the entire federal system and specific rules for practice before that court. State supreme courts perform the same function generally for the state judicial systems.

Rules of civil and criminal procedure may be and often are enacted or approved by the legislature. These rules govern important rights since they must be strictly adhered to in order to enforce or protect any rights. While complex pleading rules and writs of the past centuries no longer control litigation, they still are said to rule us from the grave. Thus, valid complaints initiating a lawsuit must state facts sufficient to make out a prima facie cause of action. Motions against the pleadings must be filed timely. Joinder of parties may be essential. Time limitations for responses to pleadings may result in final judgment.

14.1 <u>State Rules of Court.</u> The general rules for practice in any given state are located in each state code. If the code is annotated, the court interpretation will also be included. Rules of court may also be published with the bound state appellate court reports and in the regional reporter of the <u>National Reporter System.</u> In addition, many states have local practice and procedure treatises published commercially that contain the rules, annotations, and commentary on the local practice rules. The local practice treatises and state codes usually provide sample procedure forms.

14.2 <u>Federal Rules of Court.</u> The U.S. Supreme Court has general power to promulgate general federal rules of procedure, and may supplement and amend them as it chooses. Its rule-making authority is based upon the original Congressional enabling act and is governed by the Constitution. However, the Supreme Court procedure insists that the application of the rules "really regulates procedure, -- the judicial process for enforcing rights and duties recognized by substantive law and for justly administering remedy and redress for disregard or infraction of them." Sibbach v. Wilson Co., Inc., 312 U.S. 1 14 (1941).

The Federal Rules of Civil and Criminal Procedure, as well as the Federal Rules of Evidence, are printed in the advance sheets of all federal court reporters. They are also printed in pamphlet form by the Court. The federal rules appear in many different commercially published sources, including the annotated versions of the United States Code, U.S. C.A. and U.S.C.S. There are several treatises on the federal civil rules, including <u>Moore's Federal Practice,</u> <u>West's Federal Practice Manual,</u> and <u>Federal Rules Digest and Service,</u> as well as the evidence and criminal procedure rules.

In addition to the general rules of procedure, each court also published rules of practice before the individual court. These can be obtained directly from the clerk of the court, and govern such matters as motion days and assignment of cases.

Chapter 4

PERSUASIVE AUTHORITY

15 USE OF PERSUASIVE AUTHORITY

In many cases the lawyer or researcher does not find any specific cases, statutes, or administrative regulations dealing directly with a given fact situation. It may be that the issues presented are novel or arise in peculiar circumstances. The issues may arise in the course of planning for future problems. It is likely, however, that the legal doctrines sought to be applied are unsettled and proper application is speculative. In other occasions the issues may arise because of a new statute or court decision that expressly or implicitly leaves the area of law open and undefined so that the law must develop on a case by case basis -- the specific guidelines to a general principle of law remain thus unknown.

While the lack of specific rules is confusing to the layman, an attorney or judge must act when a problem is presented. Each must rely upon his own analytical prowess, formulating a tentative conclusion that he more or less supports by fundamental reasons and arguments suggested by public policy, analogy to other areas of law, justice, dictum, and common sense. These tentative conclusions are then researched in the secondary sources for additional support. These secondary authorities are the authors of legal periodical articles and notes, and of the legal treatises on law, and of books on subjects related to law such as materials written in the social science areas. These secondary sources are then cited as supporting the argument made. Of course, as in all areas of legal research, a constant evaluation must be made of all conclusions during the process of research, depending upon what is found, so that theories often change according to the weight and value of precedent, primary authority, or secondary authority located.

One additional, and very important, use of the scholarly writings in law journals and treatises is to reshape the law where bad rules have been adopted, ill-conceived legislation has been enacted, or unconstitutional laws are in force. Creative lawyers, judges, and legislators use the criticism in the legal journals and

treatises to reformulate unsound, unwise, or unjust rules.
Thus, though there may be adequate authority for a proposition
in existing statutes or decisions, those statutes and decisions
may be attacked and struck down by enterprising counsel.

16 LEGAL PERIODICALS

There are basically four types of legal periodicals, the
most important of which for scholars is the university law
review or law journal. The university law review or law journal
is a publication by the students of the many law schools. The
third-year students control the editorial process and select the
articles, notes, and case comments to be published. Second-
year law students perform the tiresome, but necessary, task
of checking the accuracy of all sources cited. A piece submitted
to a student-run law review seldom emerges from the cite
checking and editing process looking the same as it entered.
Traditionally the students yield each piece to rigorous editorial
scrutiny by at least four different editors who delight in attacking
each word, clause, phrase, sentence, paragraph, and section to
excise any conceivable substantive or stylistic error. The typical student law review consists of leading articles normally
written by judges, lawyers, and law professors, notes or comments on a particular narrow legal subject by third-year law
students, case notes or case comments on a leading court decision by second-year students, and book reviews by judges,
lawyers, and law professors. The subjects covered in the typical
law review are not normally related at all. From time to time,
however, the law review will feature a symposium on a single
topic, or will present a review of the local legislation or court
opinions, or a review of the circuit opinions from the court of
appeals and the leading federal district courts.

Another type of legal periodical is the professional journal
from the professional legal societies. The American Bar As-
sociation has both its general publication, the American Bar
Association Journal, and the publications from its many sections,
such as the Antitrust Law Journal published by the American
Bar Association Section of Antitrust Law. In addition to the
American Bar Association, the Association of American Law
Schools publishes the Journal of Legal Education; the Judicature
Society publishes Judicature; the American Trial Lawyers Bar
Association publishes the American Trial Lawyers Journal;
and state bars publish journals.

A wide number of daily or weekly law practice periodicals and legal newspapers are published in the major cities and in some large counties. The quality of articles is much lower in these publications, which are largely aimed at routine legal practice. An example is the Los Angeles Daily Journal, or the Salt Lake City Daily Record.

A fourth type of legal periodical is the weekly or monthly news letters published commercially and usually confined to a single topic. The most significant of these periodicals is the U.S. Law Week service published by the Bureau of National Affairs. Law Week contains three major services; new federal statutes of immediate interest, latest decisions of general interest from the lower federal courts and the state courts, and the orders and opinions of the Supreme Court. The General Law section consists of two parts: a brief summary and analysis of four to eight pages that briefs the important state and lower federal court cases, and a section covering new court decisions, federal agency rulings, and special articles dealing with matters of general interest to the legal profession. The Summary and Analysis section cites to the decisions partially reported in the Decisions section. In addition, there is a general topical index and a table of cases and orders to this General Law section. The Supreme Court sections contain the basic journal of the Court, summaries of the orders, cases docketed, and hearings scheduled. In additon, in a separate section, the opinions of the Court are reported in full. A separate index section contains a topical index, a table of cases, and a docket numbers table. The value of the U.S. Law Week, as discussed at ¶ 6.2.3 and 6.2.7, supra, is the fact that it is the only source for judicial opinions for up to six months because of the slowness of the advance sheet digesting system.

16.1 The major legal periodicals are indexed in the Index to Legal Periodicals, advised by the American Association of Law Libraries. The method of selection of the journals to be indexed in the ILP is based upon whether the journal regularly publishes articles and notes of legal content of high quality and permanent reference value. Articles are indexed by author, if the author is not a student, and by subject (not by title). For example, an article by Senator Barry M. Goldwater, entitled "President's Constitutional Primacy in Foreign Relations and National Defense," appearing in volume 13 of the Virginia Journal of International Law, at page 463, is listed as follows:

GOLDWATER, Barry M.
　　Executive power (P)
　　US: foreign relations (P)
　　US: President (P)

EXECUTIVE power
　　President's constitutional primacy in foreign
　　relations and national defense. B.M. Goldwater.
　　Va J Int L 13:463-89 Summer '73

UNITED STATES: foreign relations

　　President's constitutional primacy in foreign
　　relations and national defense. B.M. Goldwater.
　　Va J Int L 13:463-89 Summer '73

UNITED STATES: President

　　President's constitutional primacy in foreign
　　relations and national defense. B.M. Goldwater.
　　Va J Int L 13:463-89 Summer '73

In addition to the article and note or comment index by subject,
the ILP also indexes cases noted in a section called Table of
Cases Commented Upon. A typical entry is as follows:

　　FUENTES v. Shevin, 92 Sup Ct. 1983
　　　Baylor L Rev 25:215-55 Spring '73
　　　Chi-Kent L Rev 49:229-243 Fall-Winter '72
　　　Com L J 78:283-8 Ag '73
　　　Creighton L Rev 6:410-16 '72-'73
　　　Loyola L Rev 19:530-41 '72-'73
　　　Va L Rev 59:355-409 Mr '73

The final part of the ILP indexes is the Book Review Index. A
typical entry is as follows:

　　DOUGLAS, William O.
　　　Points of rebellion. 1970
　　　　G.S. Grossman. Utah L Rev 1970:302 Ap '70

The subject arrangement of the Subject and Author Index in ILP
is difficult to use because of the lack of sufficient cross reference and the translation problems of law to layman's language.
Considerable ingenuity must be used to insure full searching of

the Index to Legal Periodicals, and its companion indexes, Index to Foreign Legal Periodicals, and the Mersky & Jacobstein Index to Periodical Articles Related to Law (Glanville Publishers, Inc.). The abbreviations used in identifying the name of the law review or journal are listed in the front of each index. The key to the sample author entry listed above is that the letters in parentheses under the author's name refer to the first letter of the title of the article under the listed subject headings. Checklist of Anglo-American Periodicals by L.B. Morse (Glanville Publishers, Inc.) affords volume listing and pagination on major legal periodicals.

17 LEGAL TREATISES

The legal treatises are books written by professors of law, judges, or lawyers, on specific legal subjects. For example, Professor Grant Gilmore published a two-volume treatise on the financing and mortgaging of property other than real estate; a citation to a section in his books would be: G. Gilmore, Security Interests in Personal Property § 14 (1965). There are legal treatises on nearly every subject in the law. They are written for the use of practising lawyers and judges to aid them in understanding the statutes, court decisions, administrative regulations, and the history of the subject. In addition to an explanation of the primary sources of law, the author will frequently criticise the current rules of law and suggest logical changes based upon careful reasoning and analysis.

In addition to the assistance that treatises give to the lawyer in advising his client or formulating the basis for an action or defense, the courts frequently rely upon the treatises, not so much as a source of authority, but because of the carefully reasoned conclusions from an apparently unbiased commentator on the law. Not all treatises are accorded the same weight by the courts, and care must be taken in selecting the most widely respected treatises.

Treatises may be used as one would use any book: most have a very sophisticated index, a table of cases cited or discussed in the text, a table of contents, and most importantly for lawyers, supplementation. The supplementation may consist of annual pocket parts inserted in the front or rear of the book, or the book may be in looseleaf binders, and the individual pages that are changed are removed and replaced with new pages. The supplementation normally consists of new cases and new statutes, commentary on important changes in the case law or statutes and footnote citations that would accompany new text if the entire book were reprinted.

There are many specialized treatises which are more correctly classified as form books, procedure and practice books, the ALI Restatements of the Law, general theory books such as those published in the philosophy of law area, etc. These specialized books will be mentioned in the practical application section of this book in connection with the subjects research discussion. Law Books in Print by Jacobstein and Pimsleur, as updated by Pimsleur's Law Books Published (both Glanville), is an outstanding source for locating texts and treatises.

18 USING THE LAW CARD CATALOG

There are two basic schemes for finding treatises and other cataloged materials in the law library, or the law portion of a general library. Most libraries now follow the generally accepted method of arranging books on the shelf by subject. This means that if one is looking for books on the law of contracts, locating one book about contracts on the shelf will also locate other books on contracts, leases, commercial agreements, secured financing, bills and notes, etc. The other approach is to locate the book in the card catalog. This is a simple task if either the author or title of the treatise is known. If, however, the books to be located must be located by subject only, there is some difficulty finding books by subject. Librarians and catalogers often have difficulty selecting the proper subject headings for the books they catalog. A book on real estate foreclosure would logically fall under a number of subjects: real estate, land law, land finance, mortgages, trust deed forclosure, judicial sale of real property, real property, secured financing, civil procedure, etc. The lawyer may look under each of these title subjects, only to discover to his dismay that the librarians have classified the book under "Sales -- land." The subject card catalog in the library must be used with some care and ingenuity. It can be a very fruitful source of information. Often the novice to the law would be best advised to begin the legal research in the treatises once the categorization of the legal problem into its proper legal subject has taken place.

19 GOVERNMENT DOCUMENTS -- MAKING SENSE OF THE DOCUMENT SYSTEM

While access to primary legal sources and supporting documents of the United States has been discussed (see 10, 12, and 13), the arrangement of the documents collection in a large depository library or a large law library can be very confusing. In brief review, the primary federal law comprises laws of the United States, regulations promulgated by the administrative agencies pursuant to the laws of the United States, executive orders of the President, treaties of the United States, resolutions of the Congress, proclamations of the President, and of course, the Constitution of the United States. In addition to the books containing these basic law documents, there are many thousands of books, pamphlets, and serials published by the United States and distributed by the Government Printing Office or by the issuing agency. Many of these publications are located in U.S. Government Depository libraries. There is usually at least one depository library in each major city as well as at the major universities and major law libraries.

19.1 Location and Arrangement of Documents. In the law libraries, normally the significant primary sources are located in the major working part of the reference library -- close to the central reading room and reference desk. Thus, such items as the U.S. Code, the Statutes at Large, Code of Federal Regulations, and current tables and indexes to these sets will be separated from the basic documents collection, as will be the official U.S. Reports of the United States Supreme Court and the advance sheets to U.S. Reports. These primary items will be best located by asking at the main reference or circulation desk in the law libraries. The supporting documents to the primary materials in the law libraries will probably be located either in a separate document collection using the classification system developed for use in the Library of the Public Documents Department, or in the regularly classified collection, which may be the Library of Congress classification scheme, the Dewey decimal system, or a self-developed system.

Primary sources in the general library will be located in the documents collection either in the documents classification scheme or in the general collection under the Library of Congress, Dewey, or a self-developed scheme. General libraries, as well as law libraries, frequently employ a professional librarian to develop and maintain the documents collection, as well as to give reference service.

19.2 Use of the Monthly Catalog as an Index. Publications available to the public are listed as published in the Monthly Catalog of United States Government Publications, issued by the

Superintendent of Documents, U.S. Government Printing Office, Washington, D.C. 20402. The publications are arranged according to the general administrative department, alphabetically by department, and are assigned an entry number. For example, the publication "Resource List for Drug Abuse Literature" is listed under the subheading "Narcotics and Dangerous Drugs Bureau," which is listed under the general department heading, "Justice Department." The entry number for this publication is 23666 and is located on page 79 of the May 1973 issue of the Monthly Catalog. The complete entry is as follows:

NARCOTICS AND DANGEROUS DRUGS BUREAU,
Justice Dept., Washington, DC 20530

23666 Resource list for drug abuse literature. (Jan. 1, 1971)
(5) p. 4 ° † + 24.12:R31

This publication is not automatically sent to all depository libraries. The small dagger indicates that distribution is made by the issuing office. If the particular library did have this publication, its location would be under the documents classification call number of J24.12:R31 if the library is using the documents classification system. In addition to being located under the administrative agency issuing it, this publication is also listed in the index in the back of the Monthly Catalog. It is listed under the general heading of "drug abuse" as follows:

Drug abuse:
   alcohol and drug abuse, interchange, lessons
     learned and other information, 22431
   clinical recognition and treatment, etc.,
     22433
   drugs in our schools, hearings, 23009
   resource list for drug abuse literature,
     23666

The key referencing number is the five digit number, 23666. All publications in the Monthly Catalog are given an entry number, such as 23666. The numbers run consecutively at the left margin of each publication. All U.S. government publications can be located in the Monthly Catalog system, although the name changes during the earlier years. The Monthly Catalog makes no attempt to abstract any information about the document.

    19.3 The Congressional Information Service Index System.

The difficulty of doing substantive legal research in the legislative history documents published by the Government Printing Office (herein after GPO) has been partially alleviated by the publication of the Congressional Information Service Abstracts and Index. The system makes a general abstraction of each hearing report or committee report and then indexes by name of participant (witnesses) and by general subjects discussed. This will be useful for generalized research, but the lawyer's need is to find detailed discussion of individual sections of major legislation. It is the interpretation of the particular language of a federal law that requires searching the hearings and reports. The CIS system cannot do this particularized searching. It is very useful, however, as an initial starting point and for eliminating obviously irrelevant documents.

19.4 Arrangement of Government Documents on the Shelf. The documents classification system arranges the documents on the shelf first by major department, such as Commerce Department, or Housing and Urban Development, and then subdivides the department into divisons and then arranges the documents by subject. It is possible to go directly to the shelves and locate documents by finding the appropriate agency and then searching each item in the appropriate subject group. Since lawyers tend to avoid catalogs and indexes, some law libraries break out the major publications from the documents system and arrange them by subject on the shelves with the treatises and monographs. This way, lawyers and law students stumble into these normally separate books. Thus, for some libraries, one must look in the card catalog as well as in the Monthly Catalog, or better, ask the reference librarian for the documents collection for help.

Chapter 5

RESEARCHING IN SPECIFIC FIELDS OF LAW

20 GENERAL CONSIDERATIONS

Throughout the first four chapters of this book, each of the major research systems has been explained generally. However, simply explaining a system in the bibliography field is not sufficient to prepare a student of the subject to do either the mechanics of research, or to proceed with substantive research. The materials that follow are detailed guides for performing the research necessary for the subjects presented. Each subject will follow a basic checklist, which is illustrated below:

> (1) Is a statute, code, or ordinance involved?
> (2) What have the courts said about the subject?
> (3) Is there any commentary available about the subject?
> (4) Update all research.

Preliminary to any intensive research, however, as indicated in Chapter 1, is the necessity of locating the proper subject field and then narrowing the search to the proper topic and subtopic in that major field. For the lawyer, this step is normally not necessary; for the advanced law student, this step may be necessary; for the beginning law student and the novice to law, this step is absolutely necessary.

One caution to laymen and novices in the law: through experience, I have frequently found that general students are not prepared for the magnitude of research necessary to resolve favorable a complicated legal question. Often, the questions being examined by laymen and the general student are quite broad and the answer being sought is a general statement of the general rules. On the other hand, lawyers and law students seek for the very narrow application of the general rule to specific fact situations. Specific issues raised by fact conflict are resolved not by reference to some general proposition of law, but by careful comparison with particular statutory language or comparable fact situations in court decisions. The index tools and treatises of the law library are geared to specific fact-created issues, and not to general problems of society, although there is a good deal of commentary available about the general problems in the legal system and in the rules of law. Thus, to locate a general proposition of law about the free will of man, the general student should not begin by searching statutes and case law, but with scholarly books or law review articles that address themselves to the general question of free will. Thus, it is probably more advantageous for the general student to begin researching first in the general library, either community or university, before going to the local bar association library or university law library.

21 RESEARCHING ENVIRONMENTAL LAW

Environmental law is a new subject area in the law, but some of the private citizens' rights are as old as the common law. The major thrust of environmental litigation, however, has been in the area of citizens' suits against the federal agencies under the various federal environmental protection statutes, principally the National Environmental Policy Act (NEPA). In addition, there has been a great deal of flurry over the federal clean air and clean water statutes requiring the states to enact laws meeting certain minimum standards. The goal behind the clean air and clean water statutes is that the federal government will step in and by regulation force the states to clean up their environment. This same mechanism is also at work in urban planning, noise, and sanitation statutes.

21.1 Locating the applicable statute. The most basic and essential research tool for locating the applicable statutes (and cases) dealing with both the federal laws and state laws is the following set:

Bureau of National Affairs. Environment Reporter. 11 vols.
This set is looseleaf, and is supplemented weekly with new cases, laws, regulations, articles, etc.

The volumes necessary to find applicable federal statutes are (1) the volume marked "Federal Laws" and (2) the volume marked "Federal Regulations." In addition to the text of each statute, there is also very helpful commentary, legislative history, presidential orders, etc., to assist in understanding the current state of the law.

The basic federal statutes and their locations are as follows:

The National Environmental Policy Act, Pub. L. 91-190, effective Jan. 1, 1970; 83 Stat. 852, codified at 42 U.S.C. §§4321, 4331-4335, 4341-4374 (1970).

Environmental Quality Improvement Act of 1970, Pub. L. 91-224, title II, §§ 202-205; 84 Stat. 114, codified at 42 U.S.C. §§4371-4374 (1970).

Clean Air Act, amended, codified at 42 U.S.C. §§1857 et seq. (1970).

Solid Waste Disposal Act, as amended, codified at 42 U.S.C. §§ 3251-3259 (1970).

Federal Water Pollution Control Act, as amended, codified at 33 U.S.C. §§ 1155, 1157, 1158, 1251-1265, 1281-1292, 1311-1328, 1341-1345, 1361-1376 (1970).

Rivers and Harbors Act of 1899, codified at 33 U.S.C. §§ 401-413 (1970).

Noise Control Act of 1972, codified at 42 U.S.C. §§4901-4918; 49 U.S.C. §1431 (1970).

Federal Environmental Pesticide Control Act of 1972, 86 Stat. 973, codified at 7 U.S.C. §§136-136y, 15 U.S.C. §§ 1261, 1471, 21 U.S.C.§§ 321, 346a (1970).

There are other major acts in addition to these, but these are the most significant to the general public. There are hundreds of pages of federal regulations having the force and effect of law, which are located at title 40, Code of Federal Regulations. The major source of federal regulations for the environment is the Environmental Protection Agency (EPA).

The state statutes are located in the BNA, Environment Reporter, and are also available in each individual set of state laws, or state codes. Since each major state statute will follow similar subjects as the main federal statutes listed above, search in the code index for such topics as water pollution, water quality, air quality, and noise standards.

28.2 Locating the applicable court decisions. The looseleaf up-to-date method of searching for court decisions is the following set:

Bureau of National Affairs. <u>Environment Reporter</u>. 11
vols. This set is looseleaf, and supplemented weekly
with all new cases, both state and federal, dealing with
issues relevant to environmental considerations.

The volumes necessary to find applicable state and federal cases
are (1) the looseleaf volume marked <u>Decisions</u>, and (2) individual
volumes entitled <u>Environment Reporter -- Cases</u>. The proper
citation to the <u>Environment Reporter Cases</u> is as follows: 5
E.R.C. 579 (court of decision and date).

A more traditional method of searching for any case law is
through the digest systems available. The <u>Environment Reporter</u>
uses its own index digest system. Searching in this set for cases
on a particular subject involves first, going to the topical index
to locate the digest § numbers that are applicable, and second,
locating the particular subsections of the subject under the
classification guide, and third, reading the headnotes in the index
digest. For example, looking for a case discussing the application
of the NEPA to highway construction, the topical index under
"Highways" shows "Regulation § 8.353." The classification
guide shows that this is in the digest topic "land, subdivision,
Federal, state and local regulation -- highways." Scanning the
index digest under § number 8.353, we find that there are a number
of federal district court decisions, as well as courts of appeals
decisions, that required full and complete compliance with NEPA
so long as the project was ongoing when NEPA was enacted, and
the cost of altering or abandoning the project do not clearly
outweigh the environmental considerations. <u>Scherr</u> v. <u>Volpe</u>,
4 E.R.C. 1435 (7th Cir. 1972).

The West Key Number Digest system uses a number of
different and somewhat confusing topics to locate an integrated
and complex environmental law case. Under the topic of "pollution" in the cumulative supplement volume of the <u>Descriptive
Word Index</u>, the following different key numbers and subjects are
listed:

> Courts 379
> Corporations 306
> Health and Environment 25.5, 25.10
> Highways 103
> Fines 21
> Courts 299.3
> Courts 277.2

Since most of the significant environmental law cases are being

tried in the federal district courts, and appeals have not gone any
further than the courts of appeals, the best beginning digest is
the West's Modern Federal Practice Digest, beginning with the
most recent supplements, since the law is so new. For larger
states, such as California or New York, it m   be wiser to begin
with the local state digest before going to the Environment Reporter or the federal digest system.

    21.3 Locating relevant commentary. There are a number of
very good general legal treatises on the environment, and there
is an extensive amount written in the law reviews. In addition
to strictly legal materials, there are mountains of nonlaw sources
for research in environmental questions since it is a problem that
crosses the disciplinary boundaries. The significance in the amount
of sources other than law that is available is reflected in Professor
George S. Grossman's very fine bibliography: Bibliographical
Control in Law and the Environment -- Surviving an Explosion.
Council of Planning Librarians, 1971. 27 p. Z/5942/.C68/No. 134.
The remainder of the information about books or periodicals
listed below is restricted to law.

    Environmental materials on law are located at these general
Library of Congress call numbers: HC/107, KF/2125, KF/8925,
KF/3812, KF/3775, K/E5, HC/110/.E5, TD/180, and other numbers
as indicated in the library card catalog.

    The Martindale-Hubbell Law Directory, volume 5, lists under
each state the pertinent state statutes or case law (if developed)
for that state. Each state is listed alphabetically with a digest of
each state's general laws. These state digests consist of about
fifty pages each with only general topics discussed in several
short paragraphs. Environmental law topics are all grouped
together under the topic "Environment." However, since many
different legal doctrines may come into play in environmental
litigation, other topics should be checked, such as "Water
Rights," etc.

    The following is a listing of books specifically on the
environment or that have relevant sections on the environment:

    BNA. Energy Users Report. 3 vols. looseleaf, updated weekly.
      1973.

    Davis, Kenneth C. Administrative Law Treatise. 5 vols. St.
      Paul: West Publishing Co. 1970. Deals with general admini-
      strative problems relevant to the procedures created by
      NEPA and other environmental statutes.

    Grad, Frank P. Treatise on Environmental Law. Vol. 1.
      New York: Matthew Bender. 1973. (Other volumes forth-

coming)

Henke, Dan. California Legal Research Handbook. Walnut Creek, California: Lex-Cal-Tex Press, 1971. KF/240/ .H4/C.3 See 17.19-E61. Discussion focuses on environmental law materials for California, as well as broader sources.

Krier, James E. Environmental Law and Policy. New York: Bobbs-Merrill. 1971.

PLI. Legal Control of the Environment. New York: Practising Law Institute. 1972.

PLI. Pollution and Industrial Waste. New York: Practising Law Institute. 1970.

Powell on Real Property. New York: Matthew Bender. 1973. See ¶ s 716, 722, 725, and 726 (water pollution).

Prosser on Torts. St. Paul: West Publishing Co. 1972. See Nuisance.

Sax, Joseph L. Defending the Environment. New York: Knopf. 1971.

Sloan, Irving J. Environment and the Law. Oceana Legal Almanac Series No. 65. Dobbs Ferry, New York: Oceana Publications, Inc. 1971.

Yannacone, Victor J. & Cohen, Bernard S. Environmental Rights & Remedies. Rochester, New York: Lawyers Coop & Bancroft-Whitney. 2 vols. 1973.

Zwick, David. Water Waste-Land. New York: Bantam. Ralph Nader Study Group on Water Pollution. 1971.

In addition to these books, the U.S. Government Printing Office has published a number of very useful items, which are listed in the Monthly Catalog. Among those of interest are hearings of the various committees of Congress, some of which are located at Y4.C73/2:En8/5/. In addition to the regular studies done by the government, the Environmental Protection Agency has published several feet of useful documents, located at EPI et seq. Note that the EPA has printed various bibliographies with abstracts such as:

Noise Facts Digest. EPI.30:972.

Odors and Air Pollution: A Bibliography with Abstracts. EP4.9:113 (1972).

Law Review articles should be searched through the Index to Legal Periodicals, as well as the Jacobstein and Mersky Index to Periodical Articles Related to Law. Two publications have reprinted significant law review articles:

Environmental Law. Edited by Research and Development Corp. Greenvale, N.Y. 1970.

Environmental Law Review. New York: Clark Boardman
Co. vols. 1-4 currently printed, vol. 5 expected in 1973.

22 RESEARCHING CONSUMER LAW AND BANKRUPTCY

This discussion focuses primarily on the rights of the
debtor consumer. Debtor means the person owing a debt. The
person expecting payment is the creditor. A number of laws have
been enacted, with no small fanfare from legislators, to protect
the rights of the consumer, but few have any practical utility
to the individual consumer. The highly touted truth-in-lending
legislation does not seem to have actually benefited the average
consumer. Those who previsouly fell prey to loan sharks are
still bad credit risks, and continue to seek out the high risk
lenders who exceed the statutory limits for credit.

22.1 Locating the applicable statute. The bankruptcy law
of the United States is vested exclusively by the Constitution
in the federal government. The federal Bankruptcy Act, as
amended, is located as follows:

Bankruptcy Act, 11 U.S.C.§§1 et seq. (1970).
The West publication United States Code Annotated, will also
help you locate relevant case law applicable to each section of the
act. Frequently the Bankruptcy Act, or relevant portions thereof,
will be printed in business law books or business law statutory
supplements. The best such supplements are as follows:

> Nordstrom, Robert J., and Clovis, Albert L. Selected
> Commercial Statutes. St. Paul: West Publishing Co. 1974.
> Countryman, Vern, and Kaufman, Andrew L. Commercial
> Law Selected Statutes. Boston: Little, Brown and Co.
> 1971.

The other important commercial statutes dealing with consumers'
rights, or with which consumers should be familiar are as follows,
also locatd in the above two cited works:

> Uniform Commercial Code. This act has been adopted in
> all the states except Louisiana, which has a similar
> statute. The basic sections applicable to consumers are
> Articles I, II, III, and IX. The important provisions are
> the sections on conscionability of sales agreements,
> implied warranties, self help remedies, and the require-
> ment of honesty in fact.
> Consumer Credit Protection Act of 1968, as amended, 15
> U.S.C.§§1601-1655 and not to § 1601 (1970).
> Uniform Consumer Credit Code (UCCC). Adopted in some
> of the states; see local state code for enactment of this

act. Text approved by the National Conference of Commissioners on Uniform State Laws.

Uniform Consumer Sales Practices Act. Not adopted in many states; approved by the American Bar Association, and adopted by the National Conference of Commissioners on Uniform State Laws.

The text of these and similar local laws are located in the individual state codes or statutes. Because most state codes are annotated with court interpretations of the sections of the law litigated, the individual state code should be used as the basic research guide.

22.2 Locating the applicable court decisions. Case law construing the statutes, such as the Bankruptcy Act, is best located in the annotated codification of the statute, in either the U.S. Code Annotated, or the various state codes, such as the Utah Code Annotated. Each section of the particular statute will be followed by any court cases that have discussed that section. For the bankruptcy law, there are numerous court decisions on practically every section of the Bankruptcy Act. On the other hand, many of the newer consumer protection statutes have not had a great deal of litigation that appears in the reporter court decisions.

The West Key Number Digest system has a number of topics for consumer case law. Under the topic of "Consumer Protection" in the cumulative supplement volume of the Modern Federal Practice Digest Descriptive Word Index the following different key numbers and subjects are listed:

Garnishment 251
Constitutional Law 318
Pawnbrokers 9

In addition to "Consumer Protection," the topic "Consumers" has these key numbers and subjects:

Courts 263
Bankruptcy 1
Commerce 48
Sales 255
Pawnbrokers 6.1
Trade Regulation 914
Taxation 1264
Federal Civil Procedure 1699

Under the topic "Bankruptcy," the West digest system has a separate digest topic for the subject "Bankruptcy," although the Descriptive Word Index should also be searched for particular circumstances.

Use of the Quick Index for ALR (American Law Rports)

57

2d and 3d is not particularly simple for the layman. It addresses subjects generally in terms of legal characterization, e.g., a problem that a consumer faces with a contract and note for a television set may be referenced under the topics "Secured Transactions," "Chattel Mortgages," "Sales," "Warranties," "Contracts," etc. Nevertheless, with some imagination, and the use of the general index to Am.Jur.2d, ALR is a very productive source of cases and commentary for consumers' problems and bankruptcy questions.

22.3 <u>Locating relevant commentary</u>. There are several good legal treatises on the Bankruptcy Act, as well as a number of nontechnical books on bankruptcy. Much of the material on consumer protection is centered in the legal periodicals.

The major legal treatise on bankruptcy is <u>Collier on Bankruptcy</u>, 14th Ed., 16 volumes, plus a forms book and manual. It is kept up to date by looseleaf releases that come out about three times a year. The publisher is Matthew Bender & Co., Inc., Albany, New York. In addition to a very detailed discussion of the sections of the code itself, it cites thousands of cases, and provides collateral matters raised in connection with the application of the act to such areas as security interests, etc. Another major treatise on bankruptcy is:

> Remington, Harold. <u>Treatise on the Bankruptcy Law of the United States</u>. 5th-6th ed. 15 vols. New York: Lawyers Coop. Updated with annual supplements.

Materials on the bankruptcy law are located at the general Library of Congress call number KF/1524/, and individually by state, such as KFC/364 for California.

In addition to the general comprehensive treatises listed above, the following is a listing of books on bankruptcy:

> Burger, Robert E., and Slavicek, Jan J. <u>Layman's Guide to Bankruptcy</u>. New York: Van Nostrand. Reinhold. 1971.

> Nims, David E. <u>Basic Bankruptcy: Alternatives, Proceedings and Discharges</u>. Ann Arbor, Michigan: Institute of Continuing Legal Education 1971.

> Paskay, Alexander L. <u>Handbook for Trustees and Receivers in Bankruptcy</u>. New York: Matthew Bender. 1972.

> Stanley, David T. <u>Bankruptcy: Problems, Process, Reform</u>. Washington: Brookings Institution. 1972.

> Webb, Garn H., et al. <u>Creditors' Rights and Bankruptcy: Analysis and Explanation</u>. New York: Holt, Rinehart & Winston. 1970.

Articles in the legal periodicals are indexed in the <u>Index to</u>

Legal Periodicals, and other periodical indexes under the topic "Bankruptcy" and its legal related fields.

Books on the subject of consumer protection and consumer rights did not appear prevalent until the late 1960s. The following list indicates some of the books available:

Chapman, John N. and Gray, Robert P. Consumer Finance Industry: Its Costs and Regulation. New York: Columbia University Press. 1967.

Clontz, Ralph C. Truth-in-lending Manual; Text, Forms, and Compliance with the Federal Truth-in-lending Law and Regulation Z. 2d ed. Boston: Hanover. 1970.

Havighurst, Clark C. Consumer Credit Reform. Dobbs Ferry, N.Y.: Oceana Publications. 1970. (Library of Law and Contemporary Problems.)

Hogan, William E., and Warren, William D. Commercial and Consumer Transactions: Cases and Materials. Mineola, N.Y.: Foundation Press (University Casebook Series). 1972.

Kripke, Homer. Consumer Credit; Text-Cases-Materials. St. Paul: West Publishing Co. 1970.

Law Books Published, Cumulative Volume 1972. See subject topic Consumers. Dobbs Ferry, N.Y.: Glanville Publishers.

Lloyd, David. Understanding the Uniform Commerical Code, with bibliography. Dobbs Ferry, N.Y.: Oceana Publications. 1973. Legal Almanac Series No. 62.

Morganstern, Stanley. Legal Protection for the Consumer. Dobbs Ferry, N.Y.: Oceana Publications. 1973. Legal Almanac Series No. 52.

Practising Law Institute. Consumer Protection Compliance. New York: PLI. 1971.

Scher, Irving, and Lobell, Carl D. Consumer Protection. New York: PLI. 1972.

Law review articles have been written on many subjects of interest to consumers, including consumer credit, fraud, misrepresentation, false advertising, defective products, injury from faulty products, etc.

23 RESEARCHING CRIMINAL LAW AND JUSTICE

The criminal justice system developed in the materials presented below is restricted to the focus of analyses of the accusatory process, defenses to accusation, protection of fundamental rights of citizens, prosecution and conviction, and punishment. Included within the scope of research contemplated are the elements of crime, so-called victimless crimes, white-collar crimes, organized crime, and institutional crime. Excluded of necessity are crimes committed abroad and in the military service.

There are three systems of identification of proscriptions for which criminal penalties are imposed: (1) the common law crimes, (2) state and local government crimes, and (3) federal crimes. Common law crimes are based upon early English cases and judicial decisions that came to America with the colonists. State and local governments enact statutes that describe which conduct or lack of conduct shall be criminal and punishable by the state. From time to time, some local government entities may include within their statutory crimes the common law crimes. The Congress enacts the basic federal crimes and penalties, and regulatory agencies add to these basic prohibitions by their rule-making authority.

23.1 Locating the applicable statutes. The administration of criminal justice is a matter that is supposed to be primarily committed to the states. Nevertheless, Congress does have limited powers of defining offenses and penalties in connection with its legislative powers generally in order to carry out its legislative functions. Where protection of federal property or federal functions is involved, the federal government may, and does, punish concurrently with the states if the individual state chooses to punish. Double jeopardy does not apply where both the federal and state governments choose to prosecute the same acts, although several state constitutions, such as Utah, elect not to punish if the federal authorities also punish.

Before going to the specific statute, novices to criminal law should first look at either American Jurisprudence 2d, Criminal Law, or Corpus Juris Secundum, Criminal Law, the two legal encyclopedias to get an initial background.

The major criminal statutes of the United States are contained in Title 18 of the United States Code. It is divided into four parts: Part I, Crimes; Part II, Criminal Procedure; Part III, Prisons and Prisoners; and Part IV, Correction of Youthful Offenders. Not all of the criminal sanctions enacted by Congress appear in the criminal code in Title 18, however. The specific index to the U.S. Code, or the descriptive word index to U.S. Code Annotated, or the index to the U.S. Code Service (the three sets of books containing the United States Code) should be searched carefully.

An example of a criminal provision of the United States is as follows:

18 U.S.C. § 876 (1970)   (legal citation)

CHAPTER 41-EXTORTION AND THREATS

§ 876. Mailing threatening communications

Whoever knowingly deposits in any post office or authorized depository for mail matter, to be sent or delivered by the Postal Service or knowingly causes to be delivered by the Postal Service according to the direction thereon, any communication, with or without a name or designating mark subscribed thereto, addressed to any other person, and containing any demand or request for ransom or reward for the release of any kidnaped person, shall be fined not more than $5,000 or imprisoned not more than twenty years, or both.

As amended Aug. 12, 1970, Pub. L. 91-375, §6 (j)(7), 84 Stat. 777.

The state criminal statutes are located in the individual state codes. Several of the states also publish a separate criminal code, without case annotations. In addition to the state statutes, local governmental entities, such as counties, parishes, districts, municipalities, towns, townships, etc., normally are granted power by the state constitutions to enact fire, health, and safety laws that may be punitive in nature. These ordinances are usually not printed and distributed publicly unless the municipality is very large. Copies can usually be obtained from the secretary of the agency, or the attorney representing the agency. Since the criminal statutes are normally in a bad state of repair, each factual situation should be searched individually, as a number of sections of the state code may be applicable.

23.2 <u>Locating the applicable court decisions</u>. For general research in criminal law court decisions, the most up-to-date method is to use the Bureau of National Affairs <u>Criminal Law Reporter</u>, which is updated weekly from cases that will not be reported in the national reporter system for up to several months, if at all. This reporter service covers both federal and state cases, and includes the latest developments in all fields of criminal justice, including statutes, rules of procedure, reports of special study committees, etc. The <u>Criminal Law Reporter</u> is indexed by subject and by case name. The subject or topical index is quite detailed but must be used with care.

The West Key Number Digest system uses a number of major topics for crimes and criminal justice. The best and quickest entry into the digest system for criminal law research is the descriptive word index. For example, suppose the question is whether or not the girlfriend of an embezzler is guilty of the crime of aiding and abetting. Looking under the subject "Embezzlement" in the descriptive word index, you locate the following notation:

> PARAMOUR, taking embezzled money and fleeing with
> paramour, aiding and abetting. Embez 24

This reference means that cases finding the girlfriend guilty of aiding and abetting in embezzlement situations can be located at the digest topic "Embezzlement" at key number 24 in any West digest, state, regional or federal. The digest topics for criminal justice in the West system are:

> Abduction, Abortion, Adulteration, Adultery, Affray, Arson, Bigamy, Blasphemy, Breach of the Peace, Bribery, Burglary, Common Scold, Compounding Offenses, Counterfeiting, Criminal Law, Disorderly Conduct, Disorderly House, Disturbance of Public Assemblage, Dueling, Embezzlement, Embracery, Escape, Extortion, False Personation, False Pretenses, Fires, Forgery, Fornication, Homicide, Incest, Insurrection and Sedition, Kidnapping, Larceny, Lewdness, Malicious Mischief, Mayhem, Miscegenation, Neutrality Laws, Obscenity, Obstructing Justice, Perjury, Piracy, Prize Fighting, Prostitution, Rape, Receiving Stolen Goods, Rescue, Riot, Robbery, Sodomy, Suicide, Threats, Treason, Unlawful Assembly, Vagrancy

In addition to the specific topics indicated above, rules of law other than specific criminal law also apply, such as evidence, constitutional law, rules of procedure, arrest, jury, extradition, fines, forfeitures, grand jury, indictment and information, pardon and parole, penalties, and searches and seizures. Thus, re-searching the criminal law system can become extraordinarily complex because of the extensive coverage in the digests and the thousands of cases that have been decided.

23.3 Locating relevant commentary. Criminal justice has received a great deal of attention in both the legal and nonlegal periodicals. It is a subject of great interest to sociologists, psychologists, and social workers, as well as lawyers, and thus is well represented in the journals of those disciplines. In addition, many monographs and single treatises have been written about the subject. In the current literature, criminal justice has received a disproportionate share of treatment, and has led to the creation of special Criminal Justice Reference Libraries at a number of institutions, including the University of Texas Law School (which abstracts and indexes by computer) and the University of Wisconsin Law School (funded by LEAA and state agencies).

The following are treatises and individual monographs of special interest and use to the lawyer:

American Law Institute. Model Penal Code. Philadelphia: American Law Institute. Tentative drafts, proposed final draft, 1960.

Anderson, Ronald A., and Wharton, Francis. Wharton's Criminal Law and Procedure. Rochester, N.Y.: Lawyers Coop. Supplemented up to date. 5 vols.

Bailey, F. Lee. Investigation and Preparation of Criminal Cases. Rochester, N. Y.: Lawyers Coop. 1970.

Israel, Jerold H., and LaFave, Wayne R. Criminal Procedure in a Nutshell. St. Paul: West Publishing Co., 1971.

Kadish, Sanford H., and Paulsen, Monrad G. Criminal Law and Its Processes, Cases and Materials. Boston: Little, Brown and Co., 1969.

LaFave, Wayne R., and Scott, Austin W. Crinimal Law. St. Paul: West Publishing Co. Hornbook Series. 1972.

Miller, Justin. Criminal Law. St. Paul: West Publishing Co. Hornbook Series. 1934.

Packer, Herbert L. Limits of the Criminal Sanction. Stanford, Calif.: Stanford University Press. 1968.

Perkins on Criminal Law. 2d Ed. Mineola, N.Y.: Foundation Press. 1969.

Ringel, William E. Searches & Seizures Arrests and Confessions. New York: Clark Boardman. 1972.

Rubin, S. Psychiatry & Criminal Law. Dobbs Ferry, N.Y.: Oceana Publications, 1965.

Torcia, Charles E. Wharton's Criminal Evidence. 4 vols. San Francisco: Bancroft Whitney. 1972, with 1973/74 supp.

White, Bertha. Crimes and Penalties. Dobbs Ferry, N.Y.: Oceana Publications. 1970. Legal Almanac Series No. 32.

For other works on criminal justice, see Mersky, Roy M. Law Books for Non-Law Libraries and Laymen, a Bibliography. Oceana Publications. Pp. 73-75. 1969.

The Index to Legal Periodicals has the following general criminal law topics:

> Crime prevention
> Crime, Victims of
> Criminal law
> Criminal procedure
> Criminal responsibility
> Criminal statistics
> Criminology

In addition to these general topics, specific topics should also be searched, depending upon the nature of the question being researched. See also the following topics in the Index to Legal Periodicals:

Abortion	Fraud
Administration of Justice	Freedom of Association
Admissibility of evidence	Freedom of Information
Alcoholic beverages	Freedom of Religion
Autopsy	Freedom of Speech
Bail	Freedom of the Press
Bigamy	Gambling
Birth control	Grand Jury
Blood tests	Habeas Corpus
Censorship	Homicide

Checks	Impeachment of Witnesses
Child abuse	Insanity
Civil rights	Instructions to juries
Commitment	Juries
Confessions	Jurisdiction
Conspiracy	Jurisprudence
Constitutional Law	Juvenile Courts
Contempt	Juvenile delinquency
Courts-Martial	Law enforcement
Discovery	Mental health
Discrimination	Military law
Double jeopardy	Narcotics
Drunkenness	Obscenity
Due process of law	Parole
Eavesdropping	Penology
Entrapment	Plea bargaining
Equal protection	Police
Evidence	Prisons and prisoners
Extradition	Probation
Federal rules of	
criminal procedure	Public defenders
Rehabilitation of	
criminals	Verdicts
Right to counsel	War crimes
Search and Seizure	Witnesses
Self-incrimination	
Sentencing	
Sex crimes	
Sociology	
Sterilization	
Subversive activities	

The above listing was made to indicate to the researcher how complicated a legal search of the Index to Legal Periodicals can be, and how easily a topic can be overlooked. While the editors of the Index attempt to cross-reference articles, very often the only listing may be under a single subject.

24 RESEARCHING CONSTITUTIONAL LAW AND CIVIL LIBERTIES

The subject area of constitutional law is traditionally restricted to the United States Constitution and the powers of the federal government, rights of the states, and rights of the people. A leading constitutional law casebook breaks its focus into two areas: authority of government and its distribution; and rights, privileges, and immunities under the Constitution. Constitutional law is an all-pervasive subject that manages to work into every area of law. The traditional areas of research in constitutional law are questions about the powers of the judiciary, the presidency, and the Congress. These powers are specific grants from the people to the federal government. In addition to the enumerated powers of the federal branches, the federal government also has certain implied powers that have mushroomed in recent years to include regulation of nearly anything the government wishes to become involved with. In addition to the enumerated powers, such as regulation of commerce, taxation, war making, patents and copyrights, foreign affairs, postal service, and the implied powers arising from these specific powers, the Bill of Rights and the later amendments, such as the fourteenth amendment, are also studied in the context of constitutional law. However, many of the important individual liberties are also discussed in connection with the previous subject, ¶ 23, criminal law research.

24.1 Locating the applicable statutes. The best source to begin with in researching constitutional law is the Constitution itself. It is located at the beginning of every state code, and in the various editions of the United States Code. It is probably most useful in the United States Code Annotated or the United States Code Service, since in the final analysis, the language of the Constitution means only what the courts say it means.

24.2 Locating the applicable court decisions. There are four major sources for locating case decisions: The West digest system, annotations in U.S. Code Ann., annotations in U.S. Code Service, and the American Law Reports (A.L.R.) system.

West Digest System: There is a central subject for constitutional law, but since this is a very complex area, approaching research problems directly by the subject outline at the beginning of the subject "Constitutional Law" in the Modern Federal Practice Digest, or the Supreme Court Digest should be attempted only by the expert. The best approach is through the Descriptive Word Index, and it is recommended that the Modern Federal Practice Digest, rather than the Supreme Court Digest, individual state digest, or the General Digest system, be used. The principal constitutional law cases are the United States Supreme Court decisions, but frequently they leave to the lower courts in the federal system the detailed problems of how to work out the general principles they announce. After searching carefully through the descriptive word index and all the supplements to the descriptive word index, a check should then be made of local state law in the individual state digest, such as the Idaho Digest (for Idaho), to see if the local supreme court or intermediate court has acted on the problem you are researching. In addition to the central subject of "Constitutional Law" in the West system, there are also numerous other subjects that are frequently used in lieu of the central subject to index constitutionally related cases, such as searches and seizures, schools, elections, armed services, health and education, prisons, mental health, and abortions.

Annotations in United States Code Annotated (USCA): Each of the provisions of the United States Constitution are followed by a short synopsis of each case construing that provision. A number of the constitutional provisions, such as the commerce clause, or the fourteenth amendment, are followed by headnotes from thousands of cases discussing those provisions. Where this occurs, the best indexing source is the descriptive index to the U.S. Code Annotated; otherwise, important cases may be overlooked, resulting in error.

Annotations in the United States Code Service (USCS): The case note annotations in the U.S. Code Service are similar to the arrangement in the U.S. Code Annotated, mentioned above, but the U.S. Code Service does not include all of the headnotes, but uses only those headnotes that the editors feel are important and not repetitive. As with the U.S.C.A., the topical index should be consulted in addition to the specific amendment or article of the Constitution to avoid missing an important case bearing directly on the research involved.

American Law Reports (ALR): There are three direct methods into constitutional law research through the American Law Reports system. The case method is used by going directly to the United States Reports Lawyers Edition through use of a case citation. Once locating the case in the reporter (U.S.L.ed), the headnotes may be used to trace related cases in the Supreme Court Digest, or a reference may indicate a complete annotation discussing the case located in the back of the immediate volume. The U.S. Supreme Court Digest may also be used to locate specific constitutional law cases. The third referent is the Federal Quick Index and its predecessor, the ALR digest and quick index system. The quickest index to the entire ALR system for constitutional law is the Federal Quick Index, using descriptive words from the fact situation as the key search words.

Note in searching the cases for constitutional law: This area of research is generally confined to the primary source for constitutional interpretation, e.g., the cases from the U.S. Supreme Court, and the lower federal court decisions. This area of law is extremely complex and the doctrines are not easily interpreted; nevertheless, since so many cases have been decided in this area recently, a particular case very nearly in point to the research question being searched can usually be located. Thus, in this area particularly, a good deal of ingenuity should be used to insure that all bases are touched.

24.3 Locating relevant commentary. There are no real treatises on "constitutional law" per se. Probably the closest books to hornbooks or treatises that deal with all aspects of constitutional law outside of the criminal procedure realm (see ¶ 23.3 for criminal procedure) are the law school casebooks:

Barrett, Edward L., Jr., and Bruton, Paul W. Constitutional Law (4th ed.) Mineola, N.Y.: Foundation Press. 1973.

Forkosch, Morris D. Constitutional Law (2d ed.). Mineola, N.Y.: Foundation Press. 1969.

Freund, Paul A., Sutherland, Arthur E., Howe, Mark De-Wolfe, and Brown, Ernest J. Constitutional Law. (2 vols., with supp.) Boston: Little Brown. 1970.

Gunther, Gerald, and Dowling, Noel T. Constitutional Law, Cases on. (8th ed. with supp.) Mineola, N.Y.: Foundation Press. 1970.

Gunther, Gerald, and Dowling, Noel T. Constitutional Law, Individual Rights in. (with supp.) Mineola, N.Y.: Foundation Press. 1970.

Kauper, Paul G. Constitutional Law: Cases and Materials (4th ed.) Boston: Little Brown. 1972 (with supp.)

Konvitz, Milton R. Constitutional Law: Bill of Rights Reader (5th ed.) Ithaca: Cornell Univ. Press. 1973.

In addition to the casebooks and reated teaching materials listed above, there are numerous individual books written about the various elements of the Constitution such as the commerce clause, the war powers clause, separation of powers, and the Bill of

Rights. No specific books on these subjects are recommended with the exception of the following books which may be useful:

Kurland, Philip B. Supreme Court Review. Chicago: Univ. of Chicago Press. Annual. 1960-.

Mersky, Roy M. Law Books for Non-Law Libraries and Laymen. Dobbs Ferry, N.Y.: Oceana Publications. 1969. See pp. 71-73, also, pp. 6,7, 20-22.

Newman, E. Civil Liberty and Civil Rights. 5th rev. ed. Dobbs Ferry, N.Y.: Oceana Publications. 1970. Legal Almanac Series No. 13.

Seavey, Warren A., Ed. Ballantine Problems in Law. St. Paul: West Publishing Co. (section on Constitutional Law Problems).

Wright, Charles Alan. Law of Federal Courts. St. Paul: West Publishing Co. Hornbook Series. 1970.

Wright, Charles Alan, and Miller, Arthur R. Federal Practice and Procedure. St. Paul: West Publishing Co. 12 vols. with supp. 1969-.

Much of the very good material on constitutional law topics is located in the law reviews and legal periodicals, and law articles in other periodicals. The two indexes that should be checked carefully are:

Index to Legal Periodicals, such topics as: constitutional law, constitutional history, delegation of powers, equal protection, due process, discrimination, freedom of religion, freedom of the press, freedom of speech, freedom of association, freedom of information, commerce clause.

Index to Periodical Articles Related to Law (Mersky and Jacobstein).

25 RESEARCHING COMMERCIAL LAW

Commercial law considered here involves the laws regulating commercial transactions and the forms of security in financing transactions in goods and services. The principal regulatory device in commerce is now the Uniform Commercial Code, which deals with such topics as sales, secured transactions, bills and notes, checks, banking, transfer of securities, promissory notes, chattel mortgages, pledges, consignment sales, and international business transactions.

25.1 Locating the applicable statutes. The principal statute is the Uniform Commercial Code, adopted in all states but Louisiana (which has its own commercial code), which is located in each of the individual state codes. Other important commercial statutes vary from state to state. The federal laws governing this area have to do with consumer protection (discussed in ¶ 22.1 supra), but in addition regulate banks, lending institutions, and securities transfers. These laws are complex and are best located in separate looseleaf services located in larger law libraries, or specialized sections of general libraries. They may, of course, also be located in the U.S. Code and the Code of Federal Regulations.

25.2 Locating the applicable court decisions. Each of the annotated state codes will indicate applicable state decisions and federal decisions in that jurisdiction. The best method of search after exhausting the state code is the West Publishing publication coordinated from their digest system:

> Uniform Laws Annotated. St. Paul: West Publishing Company. With 1973 supplements.

Because the Uniform Commercial Code (UCC) is relatively new, many states have little case law on any of the sections, and by finding the state section applicable, going directly to the Uniform Laws Annotated, rather than the General Digest system, will locate all of the state cases applying to that particular section. The West digest system may be used for general provisions that may apply in addition to the code.

25.3 Locating the relevant commentary. There are a number of very good treatises on the Uniform Commercial Code, and commercial law in general. A bibliography of law review articles is located in the two bibliographies indicated below; in addition, the Index to Legal Periodicals as well as the Index to Periodical Articles Related to Law should be consulted.

> ABA Section of Corporation, Banking and Business Law. Uniform Commercial Code Handbook. Chicago: ABA 1964.

American Law Institute (ALI). Uniform Commerical Code 1972 Official Text with Comments. St. Paul: West Publishing Co. 1972.

CCH. Consumer Credit Guide and Secured Transactions Guide. Chicago: Commerce Clearing House. Looseleaf.

Coogan, Peter F., et al. Secured Transactions Under the Uniform Commercial Code. New York: Bender. 1963.

Duesenberg, Richard W., and King, Lawrence P. Sales and Bulk Transfers Under the UCC. New York: Bender. 1966.

Ezer, Mitchel J. Uniform Commercial Code Bibliography. Joint Committee on Continuing Legal Education of the American Law Institute and American Bar Association. 1972. (Includes bibliography of law review articles.)

Gilmore, Grant. Security Interest in Personal Property. Boston: Little, Brown & Co. 1965 (2 vols.).

Hart, Frederick M., and Willier, William F. UCC Reporter Digest. New York: Bender. 1965.

Hawkland, William D. Commercial Paper. Chicago: ALI-ABA. 1965.

Henson, Ray D. Handbook on Secured Transactions under the Uniform Commercial Code. St. Paul: West Publishing Co. (Hornbook Series) 1973.

Lloyd, David. Understanding the Uniform Commercial Code. Dobbs Ferry, N. Y.: Oceana Publications. 1973. (Includes extensive bibliography of law review articles.)

Nordstrom, Robert J. Law of Sales. St. Paul: West Publishing Co. 1970.

Shaver, Philip A. Federal Banking Laws. Boston: Warren, Gorham and Lamont. 1969.

UCC Reporting Service. Chicago: Callaghan. 14 vols. 1973.

White, James J., and Summers, Robert S. Uniform Commercial Code. St. Paul: West Publishing Co. (Hornbook Series) 1972.

26 RESEARCHING FAMILY LAW: DIVORCE, ALIMONY, SUPPORT, ADOPTION, ETC.

Family law is basically property law, but also involves deeply personal matters such as the custody of children, restraining orders against irate spouses, and criminal penalities for failure to provide ordered child support. Part of the difficulty in this area is enforcing judgments against defendants who are currently residing in another jurisdiction (state).

26.1 Locating the applicable statutes. Family law is almost entirely a matter of state law, and all applicable statutes should be readily available in the annotated state code or statutes. There are a few uniform acts recommended in this area that have been enacted by a number of states, currently the most important act is the Uniform Reciprocal Enforcement of Support Act. Others include the Uniform Act on Blood Tests, and the Uniform Act on Paternity. The statutes are generally quite detailed in scope, but annotated court cases cited at the end of each section of law should be carefully noted. The statutes that are important in this area deal with the following:

Illegitimacy: inheritance, wrongful death, workman's compensation, bastardy, blood tests, paternity, and adoption.

Marriage: rules governing marriage, including length of time for domicile, age, incapacity, blood tests, premarital counseling.

Annulment: causes, property settlements, incapacity.

Property Rights: guardians of minors, enforcement of support orders, alimony, support, separate maintenance.

Divorce: grounds, residency requirement, counseling.

Adoption: procedures, licensing of placement agencies.

26.2 Locating the applicable court decisions. Since family law is largely state law, the state annotated code will normally provide satisfactorily all relevant cases. If, however, a general question is being researched, the individual state digest (or regional digest if the state does not have a digest) should be consulted. For a general treatment of the case law, the West General Digest system may be checked, or, perhaps more satisfactorily, check for annotations in the American Law Reports system (ALR), either through Am.Jur.2d or through the ALR Digest and Quick Index.

26.3 Locating the relevant commentary. There are a number of valuable treatises and form books in his area, even though it is largely statutory, and there are many very good articles in the legal periodicals covering this sensitive area of law. Some of the representative books in this area are:

> Brockelbank, William J., and Infausto, Felix. Interstate Enforcement of Family Support. Indianapolis: Bobbs-Merrill. 1971.

> Clark, Homer H., Jr. The Law of Domestic Relations in the United States. St. Paul: West Publishing Co. (Hornbook Series) 1968.

> Krause, Harry D. Family Law--Illegitimacy: Law and Social Policy. Indianapolis: Bobbs-Merrill. 1971.

> Kuchler, Frances W.H. The Law of Support. 2d ed. Dobbs Ferry, N. Y.: Oceana Publications, Inc. 1957.

> Lindey, Alexander. Separation Agreement and Ante-Nuptial Contracts. New York: Matthew Bender. 2 vols. 1967-(updated annually, looseleaf).

> Newman, Edwin S. Law of Separation and Divorce, 3d ed. (previously Callahan, Parnell J.T.) Dobbs Ferry, N.Y.: Oceana Publications, Inc. 1970.

Topics that should be searched in the Index to Legal Periodicals include: divorce and separation, domestic relations, domicile and residence, adoption, annulment, illegitimacy, paternity, marriage, settlements, alimony and maintenance, and related subjects where legal topics cross borders, such as workman's compensation.

There are numerous kinds of taxes, but in terms of planning and research, probably the most important are the state and federal income, estate, and gift taxes. All taxes are based upon statutes, and all research must begin with a relevant section of the state or federal tax code. The difficulty in reading the complex language of the taxation statutes, and then coordinating the statutes with regulations promulgated by the supervising governmental agency, as well as finding the applicable court decisions, administrative rulings and decisions has led to the publication by several book publishers of weekly supplemented looseleaf services. These looseleaf services should be the starting point for the novice researcher in the tax field.

27.1 Locating the applicable statutes. The federal taxation statutes are located basically in the Internal Revenue Code of 1954, as amended, which is Title 26 of the United States Code. The Regulations of the Internal Revenue Service (Federal Regulations, I.R.C.) are located at Title 26 of the Code of Federal Regulations. Citations: 26 U.S.C. § 101 (1970); 26 C.F.R. § 1.1-1(a)(1) (1973).

The unamended Internal Revenue Code of 1954 is published in the United States Statutes at Large as volume 68A.

The easiest way to use the code for beginning researchers is to locate a fact description of the problem to be researched in the topical index of one of the taxation looseleaf services, such as:

Commerce Clearing House. Standard Federal Tax Reports. 14 vols., looseleaf.

Mertens, Jacob, Jr. The Law of Federal Income Taxation. Mundelein, Illinois: Callaghan & Co. 32 vols., looseleaf.

Prentice-Hall, Inc. Federal Tax Library. Englewood Cliffs, N.J. 10 current vols., looseleaf.

The state taxation statutes and cases are located in the annotated state codes or statutes. Individual state administrative regulations are normally not published in the state code, but are published separately. Prentice-Hall publishes a looseleaf service consisting of two volumes, State and Local Taxes, that includes one volume for the home state and another volume for all states. Commerce Clearing House publishes a similar service called the State Tax Guide, and the all-states guide, All-State Sales Tax Reports as well as State Tax Cases Reports. Similar state by state assistance is located in the various specialized looseleaf service, such as Prentice-Hall's Estate Planning, a multivolume looseleaf service.

27.2 Locating the applicable court decisions. The individual digests in the West system, or the ALR system may be used, but the best coordinating and updating devices are the looseleaf services, described above and in ¶ 13, supra.

27.3 Locating the relevant commentary. There are too many excellent books about the many aspects of taxation, including planning guides and forms, to list more than just a representative sample. In addition, there are literally thousands of articles on taxation in the university law school law reviews and journals as well as the specialized taxation-oriented law journals and periodicals. The other disciples in the business-oriented professions and schools have also published numerous excellent articles on taxation. Full research in the legal periodicals and the other periodicals on this subject requires searching in the Index to Legal Periodicals, Index to Periodical Articles Related to Law, and Index to Business Periodicals.

Bittker, Boris I., and Eustice, James S. Federal Income Taxation of Corporations and Shareholders. Boston: Federal Tax Press. 1971.

Chommie, John C. Federal Income Taxation, 2d ed. St. Paul: West Publishing Co. 1973. (Hornbook Series)

Ferguson, M. Carr; Freeland, James J.; and Stephens, Richard B. Federal Income Taxation of Estates and Beneficiaries. Boston: Little, Brown & Co. 1970, with 1973 supp.

Henke, Dan F. California Legal Research Handbook. Walnut Creek, California: Lex-Cal-Tex Press. 1971.§17.19-T23.

Mersky, Roy M. Law Books for Non-Law Libraries and Laymen. Dobbs Ferry, N.Y.: Oceana Publications, Inc. 1969. Especially p. 104.

Laws governing the organization, conduct, and dissolution of business entities range from simple to extraordinarily complex. The individual proprietor of the local grocery store may begin his business with a minimum of governmental interference; however, a nationwide supermarket chain contemplating doing business in several states and planning on registration of securities with the SEC and sale of those securities on the New York Stock Exchange will subject itself to numerous federal laws and regulations, as well as state and local laws. The research problems are normally in three separate categories: (1) formulation of the entity (articles of incorporation, partnership, limited partnership) and filing documents with the proper state authorities; (2) liabilities of the entity or its officers during the course of its operation and dissolution; and (3) raising of capital and ongoing capitalization (issuance of securities -- stock certificates, bonds, units, etc.).

28.1 Locating the applicable statutes. Basic corporation and partnership formation laws are matters of state law. Many of the states have enacted the uniform laws in this field: the Uniform Limited Partnership Act, the Uniform Partnership Act, and the Model Business Corporation Act. These statutes are located in the annotated state codes. In addition, a growing body of federal corporation law has been developing in recent years. Federal statutes are located in the U.S. Code. The laws regulating the issuance of securities (documents representing a share of ownership or an outstanding debt against the entity) are both federal and state. The best source of information in the use of these statutes is the various looseleaf services provided by such companies as Prentice-Hall and Commerce Clearing House. The use and advantages of the looseleaf services in this area are similar to those in the taxation area, and are described in 27.1.

21.2 Locating the applicable court decisions. The most services are the best coordinators of the various laws, regulations, and, court and administrative agency decisions. The various digests, Wests and ALR, are useful, but should be not approached immediately by novices to the field.

28.3 Locating the relevant commentary. There are many volumes of strictly law, and functional business-oriented books on the formulation and administration of corporations and other business entities. A basic list follows that is a good place for the new researcher to start.

      Henn, Harry G. Law of Corporations. St. Paul: West Publishing Company. (Hornbook Series) 1970 (2d ed.). This is probably the easiest book to understand for all-around detailed legal analysis and discussion.

      Prentice-Hall. Various looseleaf services: Corporation, 5 vols. Corporation Forms. Corporation Guide. Securities Regulation, 2 vols.

      Fletcher, William M. Cyclopedia of Corporations, and Forms Annotated, 35 vols., complete, looseleaf. Chicago: Callaghan & Co. Current.

      Cavitch, Zolman. Business Organizations with Tax Planning. 28 vols., various individual authors. New York: Matthew Bender. Current with supplements.

      Commerce Clearing House. Various looseleaf publications: Federal Securities Law Reports; Blue Sky Law Reports (state securities laws); Stock Transfer Guide; Mutual Funds Guide; SEC Accounting Rules; various stock exchange rule guides and directories.

    The Index to Legal Periodicals contains numerous references to specialized articles that should be checked. Topics include corporations, corporations: close, corporations: foreign, corporations: officers and directors, corporations: stockholders, corporations: taxation, corporations: voting, securities, bonds, partnerships, agency.

29 RESEARCHING NATURAL RESOURCES LAW: MINING, OIL AND GAS, WATER

    Mining law traditionally falls into an area known as public land law, which includes the federal mining law (1866 Act, as amended), the Mineral Leasing Act of 1920 (oil and gas, etc.), multipurpose uses such as the Taylor Grazing Act of 1934, withdrawals, and adjudication of public land disputes. The supervision of the public land is basically divided between the

Department of the Interior and the Department of Agriculture. The Interior Department works through the Bureau of Land Management (BLM) in setting up mining interests, or oil and gas interests, while the Agriculture Department works through the Forest Service, which tries to stop mining activities.

Water law involves the rules governing rights to use water. The fundamental problem at the heart of many water controversies is the federal -- state conflict over who controls water. The federal claims are based upon (1) proprietary claims arising from the ownership of the public domain and the navigation servitude, and (2) legislative claims, based upon the grants of power in the Constitution. Interstate water disputes are settled upon two grounds, equitable apportionment and interstate compacts. State and local water regulatory schemes may be (1) riparian or reasonable use for owners next to stream, (2) prior appropriation or first come, first serve, or (3) a state statutory scheme with a combination of riparian and appropriation. In addition to these questions, water law also involves pollution, which is discussed in ¶ 21, supra, public recreation rights, and a curious area: ground water, surface water, seepage water, saved water, and stored water.

29.1 Locating the relevant statutes. The federal statutes dealing with the public lands, mining and oil and gas, are basically as follows:

Mining Law of 1872, 30 U.S.C.§§21-54 (1970).

Mining Leasing Act of 1920, 30 U.S.C. §§ 181-287 (1970).

Railroad Right of Way Leasing Act, 30 U.S.C. §§ 301-306 (1970).

Mineral Leasing Act for Acquired Lands (1947), 30 U.S.C. § §351-359 (1970).

Multiple Mineral Development Act of 1953, 30 U.S.C. §§501-505 (1970).

Multiple Mineral Development Act of 1954, 30 U.S.C. §§521-531 (1970).

Materials Disposal Act of 1947, 30 U.S.C. §§ 601-604 (1970).

Common Varieties Act (1955), 30 U.S.C.§§611-615 (1970).

Geothermal Steam Leasing Act of 1970, 30 U.S.C.§§1001-1025 (1970).

In addition to these basic mining law statutes, other public land statutes of importance to mining law and oil and gas law, as well as public use, are as follows:

Pickett Act (1910), 43 U.S.C. §§141-143 (1970) (temporary withdrawal power).

Jones Act (1927), regulates the school land grants in reservations of mineral rights.

Outer Continental Shelf Lands Act (1953), 10 U.S.C §§7421-7426, 43 U.S.C.§§1331-1343 (1970).

Dawson Act (1954).

Multiple-Use Sustained-Yield Act of 1960, 16 U.S.C. §§ 528-531 (1970).

Wilderness Act (1964), 16 U.S.C.§§1131-1136 (1970).

Mining regulations and statutes, and water statutes for the states are located in the applicable individual state annotated codes, or are available from the administrative agency charged with supervising local mining, oil and gas, and water resources.

29.2 Locating the relevant court decisions. Each West's digest unit, state or federal or general, has a section on mining law, as well as separate discussions for water, environment, etc., which are readily located in the descriptive word indexes. The American Law Reports system also has a number of good annotations on this subject, including practice aids in the various supporting units of the ALR/AmJur system.

For state court decisions dealing with statutory provisions governing public resources, the annotations in the code are the best starting point.

29.3 Locating the relevant commentary. There are a few comprehensive treatises in this area, which are listed below. Individual topics can be pursued in the Index to Legal Periodicals.

Clarke, Robert E., ed. Waters and Water Rights. Indianapolis: Allen Smith Co. 1967, with 1973 supp. 5 vols.

Energy Users Reporter. Washington, D.C.: BNA. Looseleaf.

Gower Federal Mining Service; Gower Oil and Gas Service. Denver: Rocky Mountain Mineral Law Foundation. Looseleaf services.

Hemingway, Richard W. The Law of Oil and Gas. St. Paul: West Publishing Co. (Hornbook Series) 1971.

Kuntz, Eugene Oscar. A Treatise on the Law of Oil and Gas. Cincinnati: W.H. Anderson Co. 1962, with supp. 3 vols.

Rocky Mountain Mineral Law Foundation. American Law of Mining. 5 vols. New York: Matthew Bender. 1963-loose-leaf.

Southwestern Legal Foundation. Oil and Gas Reporter. 45 vols. With index vol., monthly supp., looseleaf. Dallas.

Summers, Walter L. The Law of Oil and Gas. Kansas City: Vernon Law Book Co. 1954-with 1973 supp.

Williams, Howard R., and Meyers, Charles J. Oil and Gas Law. New York: Matthew Bender. 6 vols. 1959-loose-leaf, current.

30 RESEARCHING IN PUBLIC INTERNATIONAL LAW

The subject of public international law represents a body of legal rules applied by individual national states in disputes beyond their territorial limits, as well as international arbitration and concilliation. It does not represent the philosophical study of power relationships except in the context of arms control, disarmament, and the workings of the United Nations. This subject is best left to political scientists. The study of international law in the United States involves both statutes and treaties. With the enactment of legislative or executive law, the judiciary must interpret, and thus a certain number of significant Supreme Court decisions have also been made. In addition, numerous government documents are also important, especially those issued by the State Department and the Arms Control Agency. From time to time the president has avoided the treaty process in international agreements and has simply issued an executive order, or a presidential proclamation. Thus the beginning point for research in this area is not at all simple.

The main elements of the subject, public international law, are (1) whether a state has the necessary elements of statehood or sovereignty; (2) the rights of sovereignty, as well as the liabilities and obligations; (3) rules for relations between nations; (4) jurisdiction over people, territory, and waters; (5) settlement of controversies short of war; (6) war; (7) treaties, and

(8) the United Nations. These subjects are each introduced in either of the two legal encyclopedias, Am. Jur. 2d or Corpus Juris Secundum.

30.1 Locating the relevant statutes and treaties. The statutes of the United States dealing with public international law are located in the U.S. Code. The statutes of other nations are similarly located in their major federal codification, for example, Halsbury's Statutes of England. There are several treaties series published separately. All U.S. treaties are published in the Statutes at Large, but are most useful in one of the compiled versions. Treaties in Force, published by the G.P.O., is a contemporary beginning point for treaties research. See ¶ 10.5 supra.

30.2 Locating the relevant court decisions. The American cases on public international law are located easily in the West digest systems or in the American Law Reports (ALR) digest and index and index system. The reports of the International Court of Justice are published separately, as are the decisions of the Permanent Court of International Justice.

30.3 Locating the relevant commentary. There are no major treatises on public international law that are currently up to date. There are many very fine books on various aspects of international law, some of which are listed in Roy M. Mersky's Law Books for Non-Law Libraries and Laymen. (Dobbs Ferry, N.Y.: Oceana Publications, Inc. 1969). The Index to Legal Periodicals contains numerous references to articles dealing with international law subjects. It also indexes the several law school journals dealing with international law.

A very fine agent and expert for international law materials is also the publisher of many of the current international law books, Mr. Philip Cohen, of Oceana Publications, Dobbs Ferry, New York, who may be consulted if necessary.

31 RESEARCHING IN TORTS, INCLUDING AUTOMOBILE ACCIDENTS AND PERSONAL INJURIES

Torts is a broad area covering injuries to persons, property, and relationships. Typical torts are trespassing on land, intentionally pushing another person, and personal injuries caused by the reckless automobile driver. The injury may be produced by intentional acts, negligent acts, or failure to act when under a duty to act. The law of torts covers almost all of the vexations of life caused by others, even though the same acts may also be criminal. The relief for injury is often money damages, but also may be return of property (replevin), injunction (stopping further nuisance or damages), ejectment (dispossessing a wrongful trespasser), etc. Much of the law of torts began as common law (rights not granted by statute specifically, but enforced by common law courts), but has been replaced in part by such statutory schemes as workmen's compensation, no-fault automobile insurance procedures, etc. Thus, the statutes should be checked carefully before proceeding to the common law.

31.1 Locating the relevant statutes. State wrongful death acts, workmen's compensation statutes, etc., are in the state annotated codification of laws. Procedures before the various administering agencies can be found either in the state code, or in a separate publication of the agency, which is available at a state law library or from the agency itself. Federal torts acts, maritime personal injury acts, etc., are located in the U.S. Code. Liability for injuries may be based upon violation of a statutory standard, such as driving thirty miles per hour over the speed limit, or failure to comply with an elevator inspection rule. These standards must be searched for in the topical index to the statutes in the codes of the various jurisdictions.

31.2 Locating the relevant court decisions. Since tort law is largely a matter of local concern, or strictly federal concern, either the local state digest or the federal digest should be consulted for relevant case law. If this search is not fruitful, then the General Digest system (West) should be consulted for similar case law from other jurisdictions. ALR is frequently helpful in personal injury research, as well as other areas of tort liability, such as strict liability, nuisance, and death actions.

31.3 Locating the relevant commentary. There is a variety of treatises on the general law of torts, as well as on specific areas. The following listing is merely a representative sample of some of the better known works:

Aiken, Ray J., and Clausen, Charles D. Personal Injury Commentator. 15 vols. Chicago: Callaghan. Vol. 1, 1958-current indexes.

American Law Institute. Restatement of the Law of Torts 2d. St. Paul: West Publishing Co. 1965.

Averbach, Albert. Handling Accident Cases. 8 vols. San
Francisco: Bancroft-Whitney. 1958-current supplements.

Blashfield, DeWitt C. Automobile Law and Practice. 17
vols. St. Paul: West Publishing Co. 1965-with current
supp.

BNA. Product Safety and Liability Reporter. 3 vols. current.

Frumer, Louis R., and Friedman, Melvin I. Products
Liability. 4 vols. New York: Matthew Bender. 1960-
current supp.

Green, Leon. The Litigation Process of Tort Law. Indianapolis: Bobbs-Merrill. 1965.

Green, Pedrick, Rahl, Thode, Hawkins, and Smith. Torts,
Cases and Materials. St. Paul: West Publishing Co. 1968.

Negligence Compensation Cases Annotated. 100 plus vols.
Chicago: Callaghan Pub. Co. Current indexes.

Personal Injury: Actions, Defenses, Damages. 21 vols.
New York: Matthew Bender. Looseleaf with 1973 supplements.

Prosser on Torts, 4th ed. St. Paul: West Publishing Co.
(Hornbook Series) 1971.

Woodroof, M.G. and Squillante, A.M., Automobile Liability
and the Changing Law. Dobbs Ferry, N.Y.: Oceana
Publications, 1972.

The Index to Legal Periodicals contains many references to
various problems in torts, and should be searched carefully.

32 RESEARCHING IN ANTITRUST AND TRADE REGULATION

The problems of antitrust and regulated industries involve
the free enterprise notion of competition. The theory of pure
competition is that no single buyer or seller with equal goods
should have substantial impact on the market, thus price would

be driven close to cost. The federal government has enacted laws and regulations to ensure that there is workable competition in the market place. For goods or services for which competition is destructive, such as railroads or public utilities, government regulates those industries, fixing entrance requirements, regulating consolidations, and setting rates.

32.1 Locating the relevant statutes. There are four basic federal antitrust statutes: the Sherman Act, the Clayton Act, the Federal Trade Commission Act and the Robinson-Patman Act. The Serman Act is the basic antitrust law, with the others added as needed. Section 1 of the Sherman Act prohibits contracts, combinations, and conspiracies in restraint of trade and is aimed at behavioral activities. Section 2 of the Sherman Act prohibits monopolizing, attempts to monopolize, and conspiracies to monopolize. The section 2 prohibition of monopolizing is essentially a structural offense, i.e., monopolistic power coupled with predatory acts. Section 2 attempts to monopolize are unilateral conduct offenses and are thus behavioral in nature. Section 2 conspiracies to monopolize require a duality of conduct and really overlap Section 1. Section 3 of the Clayton Act forbids tie-in sales, but applies only to commodities. Section 7 of the Clayton Act forbids anticompetitive mergers of companies. Section 5(a)(1) of the Federal Trade Commission Act gives the FTC power to halt unfair methods of competition and deceptive practices, and it may exercise this power to stop such acts in their incipiency.

All the federal statutes regulating special industries are located, along with the antitrust statutes, in the U.S. Code. State regulatory systems over utilities, etc., are located in the state annotated codes.

32.2 Locating the relevant court decisions. The important antitrust opinions are those of the U.S. Supreme Court, which may be quickly located in the Supreme Court Digest or the U.S. Supreme Court Digest. The Modern Federal Practice Digest would be perhaps more complete and more useful on individual questions since the lower federal courts are involved heavily in the difficult antitrust cases. American Law Reports is also a useful sorce for antitrust cases and commentary.

The various administrative agencies publish their decisions in such publications as the Federal Trade Commission Reports (F.T.C.), which are also published by publishers of the looseleaf services, such as BNA and CCH or Prentice-Hall. There are looseleaf services covering the various administrative agencies that regulate industries, as well as specialized reporters, such as the Public Utilities Reports and Digest (P.U.R.). The official decisions of the administrative agencies are located in most larger law libraries and in all government depository libraries, such as major university and university law libraries and large state libraries.

32.3 Locating the relevant commentary. Because of the size of business interests involved in government regulation under the antitrust laws or the regulated industries, there are many very fine treatises, looseleaf services, and periodicals devoted to this difficult and complex area of the law. A number of the major works are listed below:

Areeda, Phillip. Antitrust Analysis: Problems, Text, Cases. Boston: Little, Brown & Co. 1967, with 1970 supp.

BNA. Antitrust and Trade Regulation Report. Looseleaf. Washingtin, D.C.: BNA. current.

Callman, Rudolph. The Law of Unfair Competition, Trade Marks and Monopolies, 3d ed. 5 vols., current supplements, looseleaf. Chicago: Callaghan & Co. 1967–

CCH. Trade Regulation Reports. 5 vols. Looseleaf. Chicago: Commerce Clearing House. Current.

Oppenheim, S. Chesterfield, and Weston, Glen E. The Lawyer's Robinson–Patman Act Sourcebook. Boston: Little, Brown & Co. 4 vols. 1971.

Toulmin, Harry A. A Treatise on the Antitrust Laws of the United States. 7 vols. Cincinnati: W.H. Anderson Co. 1949–with current supplements.

Von Kalinowski, Julian O. Antitrust and Trade Regulation. New York: Matthew Bender. 10 vols. 1969–looseleaf. (part of Business Organizations series).

Search in the Index to Legal Periodicals on these topics: antitrust law, antitrust law: damages, antitrust law: foreign, antitrust law: mergers, antitrust law: special industries trades and business, economics, fees, franchising, patents, public utilities, rate regulation, radio and television, restraint of trade, trade marks and trade names, trade regulation, unfair competition, United States: Federal Trade Commission.

33 RESEARCHING PROPERTY LAW: LANDLORD-TENANT, URBAN DEVELOPMENT

Property law covers a wide variety of rules and practices governing the use of land. It includes descriptions of the various estates in land, land use planning, zoning, rights and obligations of lessor and lessee in the lease situation, land investments, construction problems, taxation, land finance, shopping centers and other multiple use developments, administrative regulations over transfers of land, title searches, escrow problems, title recording procedures, regulations over real estate syndicate securities, condominium practice, minerals, oil and gas leases, real estate insurance, mechanics liens, and real property held in trust. Each of these areas are related somewhat. In addition to the state regulation of land and its uses, the federal government is becoming more and more involved in local real estate through consumer protection laws, loan guarantee programs, and rent guarantee programs, along with attendant higher standards.

33.1 Locating the applicable statutes. The federal housing acts are primarily located in Title 12 of the U.S. Code, but they are also scattered throughout the code. The regulations of the Housing and Urban Development Department (HUD) are printed and distributed to despository libraries. Their regulations are located in the Code of Federal Regulations. State property statutes are located in the state annotated codes. In addition to the state statutes governing transactions and uses in land, local governments, such as counties and municipalities, frequently enact ordinances covering such important items as zoning, area land use planning, subdivisions, etc., which must also be checked carefully. Local ordinances are frequently available only from the secretary of the municipality, although larger local government units publish their ordinances and regulations commercially and they are available in large law libraries.

33.2 Locating the relevant court decisions. Federal cases and federal administrative cases may be located in the Modern Federal Practice Digest as well as in the reports and documents of the HUD. Much of real property law is governed by state statutes, and thus the cases construing those state statutes can best be located in the annotated state codification of statutes, such as the Utah Code Annotated (1953). Other state cases are located in

the state digest. For local state court practice on the district
court (original trial court level) level, most states do not report these cases, although a few do have reports on this level.
Since as a practical matter this is the operational level of local
property law, it may be wise to inquire of local attorneys about
the pragmatic questions in a difficult research topic in real
property law.

33.3 Locating the relevant commentary. There are numerous
practice-oriented books on real property law, many of which
are published by the state bar association in connection with the
continuing legal education program of the bar association. The
general real property books are listed below:

ALI. Restatement of the Law of Property. Philadelphia:
American Law Institute. Casner, James.

Casner, James. American Law of Property. A Treatise
on the Law of Property in the United States. 8 vols.
Boston: Little, Brown & Co. 1952, with supplements,
but currently out of print.

Burby, William E. Real Property. 3d ed. St. Paul: West
Publishing Co. (Hornbook Series) 1965.

Cribbet, John E. Principles of the Law of Property.
Brooklyn: Foundation Press. 1962.

Hagman, Donald G. Urban Planning and Land Development
Control Law. St. Paul: West Publishing Co. (Hornbook
Series) 1971.

Moynihan, Cornelius J. Introduction to the Law of Real
Property. St. Paul: West Publishing Co. 1961.

Powell, Richard R. The Law of Real Property. 10 vols.
New York: Matthew Bender, Co. 1949-with 1973 supplement. Looseleaf.

Powell, Richard R. Powell on Real Property, Abridged Ed.
New York: Matthew Bender, Co. 1968.

Sato, Sho and Van Alstyne, Arvo. State and Local Government Law. Boston: Little, Brown & Co. 1969.

Simes, Lewis M. Law of Future Interest, 2d Ed. St. Paul:
West Publishing Co. (Hornbook Series) 1966.

Simes, Lewis M., and Smith, Allan F. The Law of Future
Interest, 2d Ed. 4 vols. St. Paul: West Publishing Co.
1956-with 1973 supplements.

Smith, Chester H., and Boyer, Ralph E. Survey of the Law
of Property. St. Paul: West Publishing Co. (Hornbook
Series) 1971.

Thompson, George W. Commentaries on the Modern Law
of Real Property. 15 vols. 1957-with 1972 supplements.

34 RESEARCHING ESTATE PLANNING, WILLS, AND TRUSTS

Estate planning involves the problems of post-mortum distribution of property. The total wealth of the nation changes hands
every generation. The lawyer's concern is with the proper
drafting of the documents to distribute the wealth a client has
accumulated after the client is dead. Many planning devices
now include intervivos or living trusts and gifts prior to death to
avoid the high death taxes imposed by the state and the federal
government on estates. Of course, basic to any estate plan is
the properly drafted will. The most difficult problem in estate
planning is not really the legal issues, but more importantly,
coverting the ideas of the client into a series of written symbols
to trigger a concept of those ideas in another person. Drafting
the instruments concisely and precisely is the major problem in
estate planning.

34.1 Locating the relevant statutes. With the exception of
the federal estate and gift tax laws and regulations, the basic wills
and trusts law is governed by state law. The state statutes are
located in the state annotated code or statutes, but care must be
taken to insure that all relevant sections are found and checked.
The Federal Estate and Gift taxation statutes and regulations are
discussed in ¶27.1 supra.

34.2 Locating the relevant court decisions. The state court
decisions are often made construing sections of the wills or
trusts statutes, and are best located by reading the annotations
at the end of each section of the code. Other decisions are best
located by using the state digest. If there are no relevant state
decisions on the question being researched, the West General

Digest system may be used, or the ALR digest and annotation system may be very helpful.

34.3 Locating the relevant commentary. There are a number of good treatises in this area, as well as many outstanding specialized books written by tax experts. In addition, many law review and journal articles are listed in the Index to Legal Periodicals. Some of the general books are listed below.

ALI. Restatement of the Law of Trusts, 2d. St Paul: West Publishing Co. 1959.

BNA. Tax Management Portfolios. Washington, D.C.: Bureau of National Affairs. This mixed set of specialized articles on various aspects of estate planning is very helpful. Looseleaf, and current.

Bogert, George G. Law of Trusts, 5th Ed. St. Paul: West Publishing Co. (Hornbook Series) 1973.

Bogert, George G. The Law of Trusts and Trustees, 2d. St. Paul: West Publishing Co. 15 vols. 1965-with 1973 supplement.

Bowe, William J., and Parker, Douglas H. Page on the Law of Wills. 8 vols. Cincinnati: W.H. Anderson, Co. 1960 1973 supp.

Casner, A. James. Estate Planning, 3d Ed. 2 vols. with 11 vols. supp. Boston: Little, Brown, & Co. 1973 supplements, 1961-

Lownes and Kramer. Estate and Gift Taxes. St. Paul: West Publishing Co. (Hornbook Series) 1962.

Scott, Austin W. Law of Trusts. 6 vols. 3rd Ed. Boston: Little, Brown, & Co. 1967-with 1973 supplement.

Shaffer, Thomas I. The Planning and Drafting of Wills and Trusts. Mineola, N.Y.: Foundation Press. 1972.

APPENDICES

Appendix A

DESCRIPTION OF TYPICAL LAW LIBRARIES -- LAW SCHOOLS AND BAR LIBRARIES

Law libraries are organized to fill the needs of attorneys, judges, law professors, and law students. There are two kinds of law libraries, working law libraries and research law libraries. The working law library contains about 60,000 volumes or less. It will have in its collection the law reports from all of the United States jurisdictions, the federal statutes and codes, and most of the publications dealing with local law. It will also have some secondary sources, such as the encyclopedias, the American Law Reports, several digests, citators, and some legal periodicals. There will also be available the basic practice sets of legal treatises. The research law library may have approximately 200,000 volumes, including all American and British legal periodicals, all court reports, all state codes and session laws, all federal statutes, codes and historical materials, all practice treatises, and many scholarly books, both on current American law and historical American law.

In either the working law library or the research law library, the primary sources of law and their indexes will generally be located in close proximity to each other, and close to reading areas. Often the library personnel also will be located close to the primary sources to assist users. The primary sources of law are the statutes and decisions of the states and the federal government. The basic portion of the statutes are the federal and state codes, along with session laws and legislative history. The basic portion of the court decisions will be at least one copy of each of the units of the National Reporter System, as well as court reports predating the National Reporter System. The digests to the reporter system will normally be next to the reporters and near a table for easy reference.

The important primary sources will take the most advantageous space in the heart of the law library, and will then be surrounded by such secondary, but important, sources as the legal periodicals and the annotated law reports and encyclopedias. Also near the primary sources will be the updating tools such as the citators in the Shepard's Citations system. Close at hand at the circulating and reserve desk will be reference help, usually an experienced law librarian or an attorney. Also at the reserve desk will be the treatises most heavily used in the law library, and often, the law library's sets of the local state codes.

In addition to the primary and important secondary legal sources, all law libraries, and especially research law libraries, will have a treatise and monograph (book) collection. The method of classifying and cataloging the books varies from library to library, but usually there is a system for locating the books both by subject and by author. Most law libraries will also have a card catalog showing subjects, author and title of each monograph in the library. Many law libraries do not have the court reports or legal periodicals cataloged, and will not have a kardex (serials check-in system by alphabet) out for public use. Either look on the shelf for serials that are not cataloged, or ask to see the library's serials holdings and location list. The books cataloged in the card catalog will often also show location, such as KF 150/ 674, or 341.578, or TAX LIBRARY. Usually a bulletin board near the card catalog will explain the symbols used in the library classification scheme.

If the library has a government documents depository, these items normally will not be in the regular monograph and treatise collection, but will be shelved in a separate collection by U.S. government documents number. From time to time librarians will catalog some documents into the treatise collection to aid in usage if the item is a popular one. The entry into the documents collection is the Government Printing Office index, Monthly Catalog, a difficult index to use. When locating materials on the subject being reserarched on the shelf, it is wise to browse through the items on the shelf next to the materials located, as they frequently are on the same subject.

Many of the law libraries, if not all, do not allow borrowing privileges on most of the collection to nonlawyers or nonstudents of the law school. At best, law collections are reference collections allowing very little borrowing. The larger university law school libraries may allow patrons to borrow monographs and treatises, as well as government documents. All law libraries have copy equipment for patrons to copy materials in the public domain, as well as materials that are copyrighted so long as it fits within fair use and is reasonable. Law firm libraries generally do not circulate except to other lawyers in the building.

Appendix B

LEGAL CITATIONS

The legal profession uniformly utilizes a system of abbreviation to indicate the location of cited materials. The authoritative guide to this system is the <u>Harvard Law Review</u> publication, <u>A Uniform System of Citation</u>, 11th Ed. The system is based upon common sense and practicalities and is not difficult to understand. The most confusing part of legal citations is the abbreviations of the names of various books, reports, codes, and reviews. However, so long as all use the same abbreviations, most citations can be located by most readers without difficulty.

The basic theory for a legal citation is that it give the proper volume number, followed by an abbreviated name of the book cited to (unless an abbreviation would be confusing) including the proper series or edition, followed by the page or section or paragraph cited, followed by the date of the book. If the cited material is independent in the cited book, it must also be cited, for example, the name of a court case, or the name of a law review article. In addition, the jurisdiction of the court must also be cited. Examples of each major legal publication are given below. Confusing abbreviations should be referred to several excellent books on legal bibliography, including the books by Price and Bitner, and Pollock.

1. Statutes

    1.1 <u>Constitutions</u>. The state or federal government name is abbreviated, along with the word "article." If the citation is in a footnote, "section" is abbreviated to §; but if not in a footnote, spell out the word "section."

        U.S. Const. art. 3, § 2.
        U.S. Const. amend. IV.
        Utah Const. art. 1, § 3.
        N.J. Const. art. 2, §6.

    1.2 <u>Statutes</u>. A statute may simply be cited to the current code (official), and if helpful, the popular name and original enactment may be cited. If the law is not in the code, it may be cited to the session laws or Statutes at Large. If the law has not been printed in the session laws or the code because it is too recent, the source it is located in at the time of the writing may be cited. If the code has been amended, and the earlier code is relevant the earlier code may be referred to. Codes are cited by section or paragraph number (because pages change in each new volume) but session laws can be cited by page (because the pages always remain the same). Supplements, including picket parts, must be indicated, if that is where the relevant language is located. Municipal codes are cited like statutes.

The Death on the High Seas Act, 46 U.S.C.§§761-68 (1970) (originally enacted as Act of Mar. 30, 1920, ch. 111,§§1-8, 41 Stat. 537).

Int. Rev. Code of 1954, § 167(a).

Utah Code Ann. § 74-3-23 (Supp. 1971).

N.Y. Educ. Law § 6450 (McKinney Supp. 1970).

1.3 Regulations (Administrative). Generally the citation for administrative regulations, orders, rules, etc., are to the Code of Federal Regulations, unless not yet printed there, in which case the citation is the Federal Register. Other administrative orders and decisions, such as those from the Internal Revenue Service or the Treasury Department are cited to their own publications if not located elsewhere, such as C.F.R.

17 C.F.R. 240.15c3-1(c)(2)(ix) (1974).

Treas. Reg. §1.167(a)-1(b) (1964).

Rev. Rul. 75-175, 1965-2 Cum. Bull. 41.

2. Cases

2.1 Federal decisions. Cases decided by the federal

93

courts are currently reported officially in the United States Reports, the Federal Reporter, 2d Series, and the Federal Supplement. They also appear in many other reporters, including the Supreme Court Reporter, U.S. Law Week, Trade Cases, etc. They need not be cited to these other reporters, but parallel citations may be given if it would be helpful. If the case is not yet reported in the official reporter, it may be cited to the unofficial reporter. Official includes the advance sheets and slip decisions of the courts. The date of the case is the date the case is decided. Earlier federal decisions were reported in various named reports, as well as in unofficial reporters, such as the Federal Cases. Examples as given below. If quoting from a different page than the page the case begins on, then a jump page must be indicated.

Moragne v. States Marine Lines, Inc., 398 U.S. 375, 396 n.12 (1970).
Noel v. United Aircraft Corp., 204 F. Supp. 929 (D. Del. 1962).
Bell v. Tug Shrike, 332 F.2d 330 (4th Cir. 1964), cert. denied, 379 U.S. 844 (1964).
The Key City, 81 U.S. (14 Wall.) 653 (1871).
De Lovio v. Boit, 7 F. Cas. 418 (No. 3776) (C.C.D. Mass. 1815).
Grigsby v. Coastal Marine Service, 235 F. Supp. 97 (W.D. La. 1964), affirmed in part, 412 F.2d 1011 (5th Cir. 1969).

2.2 State decisions. Cases decided by the state courts are reported in the National Reporter System by region. Most of the states also publish an official reporter. Where this is the case, both the official citation must be given, and then the West citation given. In addition, some states publish the reports of the intermediate appeals courts, while others also publish the district and county reports (trial court opinions). Each citation must indicate the court that decided the case. If no indication is made, it is assumed that the supreme court or highest court of the state made the decision. If no official citation is given, and only the West citation is given, the name of the state must be given in parenthesis.

Vassallo v. Nederl-Amerik Stoomy Maats Holland, 162 Tex. 52, 344 S.W.2d 421 (1961).
People v. Green, 70 Cal. 2d 654, 451 P.2d 422, 75 Cal. Rptr. 782 (1969).
Canal Nat'l. Bank v. Chapman, 171 A.2d 919 (Me. 1960).
Koeninger v. Toledo Trust Co., 49 Ohio App. 490, 197 N.E. 419 (1934).
Maxwell v. O'Connor, 1 Ill. App. 2d 124, 117 N.E.2d 326, 328 (1953).
Shields v. Yonge, 15 Ga. 349 (1854); Ford v. Monroe, 20 Wend. 210 (N.Y. 1838); and Cross v. Guthery, 2 Root 90 (Conn. 1794).
Knowlton v. Fairclough, -U.2d-, 498 P.2d 102, 109 (1974), cert. denied, 43 U.S.L.W. 1692 (Apr.3, 1974).

3. Books

In citing books, the first initial of the author is given, along with his full surname. The title appearing on the title page is given. Pages may be cited, or paragraphs or sections if the work is supplemented often. Supplements and pocket parts may be cited with a reference to the supplement.

G. Gilmore & C. Black, The Law of Admiralty §1-13 at 33-36 (1957).
D. Knowlton & R. Peshell, The Quick and the Dead 368 (1974).
H. Hansen, The Law of Boots ¶ 356-35 (5th ed. supp. 1974).

4. Periodicals

In citing periodicals, the last name only of the author is given, and if a student work, no name of the author is given. The journal or review is abbreviated unless it would be confusing.

Bysiewicz, Women in Legal Education, 25 J. Legal Ed. 503 (1973).
Comment, Towards a Solution of the Jurisdictional Problem in Multi-State Federal Habeas Corpus Actions Challenging

<u>Future Restraints</u>, 1970 Utah L. Rev. 625.

All other questions concerning rules of legal citation should be referred directly to "A Uniform System of Citation."

Appendix C

LEGAL ALMANACS RELATING TO SUBJECT MATTER CATEGORIES

In the course of this volume, occasional reference has been made to a particular volume in the Legal Almanac Series appropriate to a specific subject matter category. While Legal Almanacs neither are nor aspire to be scholarly texts or treatises, they are frequently useful overviews of subject matter law. This appendix relates specific Legal Almanac titles to the subject matter categories outlined in this work.

RESEARCHING ENVIRONMENTAL LAW, Section 21,

Sloan, I.J. Environment and the Law, LA#65 1971

RESEARCHING CONSUMER LAW AND BANKRUPTCY, Section 22

Morganstern, S. Legal Protection For the Consumer, LA#52 1973
Morganstern, S. Legal Regulation of Consumer Credit LA#70 1972
Morganstern, S. Legal Protection in Garnishment and Attachment LA#66 1971
Reams, B.D. Law for the Businessman LA#29 1974

RESEARCHING CRIMINAL LAW AND JUSTICE, Section 23

Baum, F. & Baum, J., Law of Self-Defense LA#64 1970
Francis, P., How to Serve on a Jury LA#31 1953
Pearlstein, S., Psychiatry, the Law and Mental Health 2d Ed. LA#30 1967
Sussmann, F.B. & Baum. F.S., Law of Juvenile Delinquency Rev. 3rd Ed. LA#22 1968
Tierney, K., How to be a Witness LA#67 1971
White, B., Crimes and Penalties LA#32 1970
Zarr, M., The Bill of Rights and the Police LA#40 1970

RESEARCHING CONSTITUTIONAL LAW AND CIVIL LIBERTIES,
Section 24

Francis, P., Legal Status of Women LA#53 1963

Gross, H., Privacy, Its Legal Protection LA#54 1964

Jessup. L.F., How to Become a Citizen of the U.S., 4th Ed.
LA#8 1972

Lawrence, G., Condemnation-Your Rights When the Government
Acquires Your Property LA#60 1967

Newman, E.S., Civil Liberty and Civil Rights, 5th Ed. LA#13
1970

Reitman, A. & Davidson, R.B., The Election Process: Voting
Laws and Procedures LA#24 1972

Thurman, D., Right of Access to Information from the Government
LA#71 1973

Weinberg, R.D., Confidential and Other Privileged Communications
LA#61 1967

Zarr, M., The Bill of Rights and the Police LA#40 1970

RESEARCHING COMMERCIAL LAW, Section 25

Greene, L., Law of Credit 2nd Ed. LA#10 1957

Greene, L., Law of Notaries Public 2nd Ed. LA#14 1967

Lloyd, D., Understanding the Uniform Commercial Code LA#62
1973

Reams, B.D., Law for the Businessman LA#29 1974

Wehringer, C., Arbitration-Precepts and Principles LA#39 1969

White, B., Law of Buying and Selling LA#41 1969

RESEARCHING FAMILY LAW, Section 26

Callahan, P., How to Make a Will Simplified 3rd Ed. LA#2 1974

Callahan, P., Law of Separation and Divorce 3rd Ed. LA#1 1970

Jessup. L.F., New Life Style and the Changing Law LA#45 1971

Kuchler, F.H. Law of Support 2nd Ed. LA#12 1957

Leavy, M.L., Law of Adoption 3rd Ed. LA#3 1968

MacKay, R.V., Guardianship and the Protection of Infants 2nd Ed.
LA#6 1957

Weinberg, R.D., Laws Governing Family Planning 2nd Ed. LA#12
1968

RESEARCHING TAXATION, Section 27

Goldberg, P.J., Estate Planning LA#50 1960
Goldberg, P.J., Tax Planning for Today and Tomorrow LA#51
  1961

RESEARCHING LAWS GOVERNING BUSINESS ENTITIES, Section
28

Reams, B.D., Law for the Businessman LA#29 1974

RESEARCHING IN TORTS, Section 31

Francis, P., Protection Through the Law LA#55 1964
Taylor, I., Law of Insurance 2nd Ed. LA#37 1968
Thomas, E.C., Law of Libel and Slander 3rd Ed. LA#15 1973
Woodroof, M.G. & Squillante, A.M., Automobile Liability and the
  Changing Law LA#68 1972

RESEARCHING IN PROPERTY LAW, Section 33

Callahan, P., Law of Real Estate 2nd Ed. LA#4 1951
Jessup. L.F., Landlord and Tenant 3rd Ed. LA#11 1974
Kehoe, P., Law of Condominiums and Cooperatives LA#72 1974

RESEARCHING ESTATE PLANNING, WILLS AND TRUSTS, Section
34

Callahan, P., How to Make a Will Simplified 3rd Ed. LA#2 1974
Goldberg, P.J., Estate Planning LA#50 1960
Goldberg, P.J., Tax Planning for Today and Tomorrow LA#51
  1961

Appendix D

COMMON LEGAL CITATIONS AND ABBREVIATIONS

(Conforms to Harvard Whitebook)

A.   (Atlantic Reporter)
A.2d   (Atlantic Reporter, Second Series)
A.B.A.J.   (American Bar Association Journal)
A.B.A. Rep.   (American Bar Association Report)
A.L.R.   (American Law Reports)
A.L.R.2d   (American Law Reports Second Series)
A.L.R.3d   (American Law Reports Third Series)
A.L.R. Fed.   (American Law Reports Federal)
A.M.C.   (American Maritime Cases)
Ad. L. Rev.   (Administrative Law Review)
Agri. Dec.   (Agriculture Decisions)
A.F. JAG L. Rev.   (Air Force JAG Law Review)
Ala. App.   (Alabama Appellate Court Reports)
Ala. L. Rev.   (Alabama Law Review)
Ala.   (Alabama Reports)
Alaska   (Alaska Reports)
Albany L. Rev.   (Albany Law Review)
Alta. L. Rev.   (Alberta Law Review)
All E.R.   (All England Law Reports)
Am. Bankr. R. (n.s.)   (American Bankruptcy Reports, New Series)
Am. Crim. L. Rev.   (American Criminal Law Review)
Am. Dec.   (American Decisions)
Am. Fed. Tax R.   (American Federal Tax Reports)
Am. Fed. Tax R.2d   (American Federal Tax Reports, Second Series)
Am. J. Comp. L.   (American Journal of Comparative Law)
Am. J. Int'l L.   (American Journal of International Law)
Am. Jur.   (American Jurisprudence)
Am. Jur.2d   (American Jurisprudence, Second Series)
Antitrust L. & Econ.   (Antitrust Law and Economics Review)
App. D.C.   (Appeals Cases, District of Columbia)
App. Div.   (Appellate Division Reports, N. Y. Supreme Court)
App. Div.2d   (Appellate Division Reports, N. Y. Supreme Court, Second Serie
Ariz. B.J.   (Arizona Bar Journal)
Ariz. L. Rev.   (Arizona Law Review)
Ariz.   (Arizona Reports)
Ark. L. Rev.   (Arkansas Law Review)
Ark.   (Arkansas Reports)
Austl. L.J.   (Australian Law Journal)
Austl. L.J. Rep.   (Australian Law Journal Reports)
Av. Cas.   (Aviation Cases)

B.C. Ind. & Com. L. Rev.   (Boston College Industrial and Commercial
                            Law Review)
B.T.A.   (Board of Tax Appeals Report)
B.U.L. Rev.   (Boston University Law Review)
B.Y.U.L. Rev.   (Brigham Young University Law Review)
Banking L.J.   (Banking Law Journal)
Bankr. L. Rep.   (Bankruptcy Law Reporter (CCH)
Black L.J.   (Black Law Journal)
Blue Sky L. Rep.   (Blue Sky Law Reporter(CCH)
Bus. Law.   (Business Lawyer, The)

C.A.B.   (Civil Aeronautics Board Reports)
CCH   (Commerce Clearing House)
CCH Comm. Mkt. Rep.   (Common Market Reporter (CCH)
C.C.P.A.   (Court of Customs and Patents Appeals Reports)
C.F.R.   (Code of Federal Regulations)
C.J.   (Corpus Juris)
C.J.S.   (Corpus Juris Secundum)
C.M.R.   (Court Martial Reports)
Cal. App.   (California Appellate Reports)
Cal. App.2d   (California Appellate Reports, Second Series)
Cal. Jur.   (California Jurisprudence)
Cal. Jur.2d   (California Jurisprudence, Second Edition
Calif. L. Rev.   (California Law Review)
Cal. Rptr.   (California Reporter)
Cal.   (California Reports)
Cal.2d   (California Reports, Second Series)
Cal. S.B.J.   (California State Bar Journal)
Camb. L.J.   (Cambridge Law Journal)
Can. S. Ct.   (Canada Supreme Court Reports)
Can. B.J.   (Canadian Bar Journal)
Can. B. Rev.   (Canadian Bar Review)
Case & Com.   (Case & Comment)
Catholic Law.   (Catholic Lawyer, The)
Catholic U.L. Rev.   (Catholic University of America Law Review)
Chi. B. Rec.   (Chicago Bar Record)
Cin. L. Rev.   (Cincinnati Law Review)
Clev. Bar Ass'n J.   (Cleveland Bar Association Journal)
Clev.-Mar. L. Rev.   (Cleveland-Marshall Law Review)
Colo. App.   (Colorado Court of Appeals Reports)
Colo.   (Colorado Reports)
Colum. Human Rights   (Columbia Human Rights Law Review)
Colum. J.L. & Soc. Prob.   (Columbia Journal of Law and Social Problems)
Colum. J. Transnat'l L.   (Columbia Journal of Transnational Law)

Colum. L. Rev.   (Columbia Law Review)
Colum. Soc'y Int'l L. Bull.   (Columbia Society of International Law Bulletin)
Colum. Survey Human Rights L.   (Columbia Survey of Human Rights Law)
Com. L.J.   (Commercial Law Journal)
Comm. Mkt. L.R.   (Common Market Law Reports)
Comm. Mkt. L. Rev.   (Common Market Law Review)
Cong. Rec.   (Congressional Record)
Conn. B.J.   (Connecticut Bar Journal)
Conn. L. Rev.   (Connecticut Law Review)
Conn.   (Connecticut Reports)
Conn. Supp.   (Connecticut Supplement)
Const.   (Constitution)
Cornell Int'l L.J.   (Cornell International Law Journal)
Cornell L. Q.   (Cornell Law Quarterly)
Cornell L. Rev.   (Cornell Law Review)
D.C. Cir.   (Court of Appeals for District of Columbia)
Ct. Cl.   (Court of Claims)
Ct. Cust. App.   (Court of Customs Appeals Reports)
Crim. L.Q.   (Criminal Law Quarterly)
Crim. L. Rptr.   (Criminal Law Reporter)
Cust. Ct.   (Customs Court Reports)

D.C.B.J.   (District of Columbia Bar Journal)
D.C. Cir.   (District of Columbia, Court of Appeals Cases)
D.D.C.   (District Court, District of Columbia)
D.L.R.   (Dominion Law Reports)
D.L.R.2d   (Dominion Law Reports, Second Series)
D.L.R.3d   (Dominion Law Reports (Third Series), 1969-Present)
Del.   (Delaware Reports)
Del. Ch.   (Delaware Chancery Reports)
Duke L.J.   (Duke Law Journal)

E.J. Int'l L.   (Eastern Journal of International Law)
Ecology L.Q.   (Ecology Law Quarterly)
Eng. Rep.   (English Reports - - Full Reprint)
Env. L. Rev.   (Environment Law Review)
Env. L.   (Environmental Law)
Env. L. Rptr.   (Environmental Law Reporter)

F.   (Federal Reporter)
F.2d   (Federal Reporter, Second Series)
F.D. Cosm. L. Rep.   (Food Drug Cosmetic Law Reporter (CCH)
F.P.C.   (Federal Power Commission Reports)
F.R.D.   (Federal Rules Decisions)

F. Supp.   (Federal Supplement)
Fed. B.J.   (Federal Bar Journal)
Fed. Cas.   (Federal Cases)
Fed. Est. & Gift Tax Rep.   (Federal Estate and Gift Tax Reporter (CCH)
Fed. Reg.   (Federal Register)
Fed. Rules Serv.   (Federal Rules Service)
Fed. Rules Serv.2d   (Federal Rules Service, Second Series)
Fla.   (Florida Reports)
Fla. St. U.L. Rev.   (Florida State University Law Review)
Fla. Supp.   (Florida Supplement)
Ford. L. Rev.   (Fordham Law Review)
Ford. Urban L.J.   (Fordham Urban Law Journal)
Forum   (Forum, The)

Ga.   (Georgia Reports)
Ga. App.   (Georgia Appeals Reports)
Ga. L. Rev.   (Georgia Law Review)
Ga. St. B.J.   (Georgia State Bar Journal)
Geo. L.J.   (Georgetown Law Journal)
Geo. Wash. L. Rev.   (George Washington Law Review)

Harv. Bus. Rev.   (Harvard Business Review)
Harv. Civ. Rights-Civ. Lib. L. Rev.   (Harvard Civil Rights -- Civil Liberties
                                        Law Review)
Harv. Int'l L.J.   (Harvard International Law Journal)
Harv. J. Legis.   (Harvard Journal on Legislation)
Harv. L. Rev.   (Harvard Law Review)
Hastings L.J.   (Hastings Law Journal)
Hawaii   (Hawaii Reports)
Houst. L. Rev.   (Houston Law Review)
How. L.J.   (Howard Law Journal)

I.C.C. Prac. J.   (I.C.C. Practitioners' Journal)
Idaho   (Idaho Reports)
Idaho L. Rev.   (Idaho Law Review)
Ill.   (Illinois Reports)
Ill. App.   (Illinois Appellate Court Reports)
Ill. App.2d   (Illinois Appellate Court Reports, Second Series)
Ill. B.J.   (Illinois Bar Journal)
Ill. L. Rev.   (Illinois Law Review)
Ind.   (Indiana Reports)
Ind. App.   (Indiana Appellate Reports)
Ind. L.J.   (Indiana Law Journal)
Ind. L. Rev.   (Indiana Law Review)
Ind. Legal F.   (Indiana Legal Forum)

Ins. Counsel J.   (Insurance Counsel Journal)
Ins. L.J.   (Insurance Law Journal)
Ins. L. Rep.   (Insurance Law Reporter (CCH)
Inter-Am. L. Rev.   (Inter-American Law Review)
Int. Rev. Bull.   (Internal Revenue Bulletin)
Int'l. Aff.   (International Affairs)
Int'l & Comp. L.Q.   (International and Comparative Law Quarterly)
Int'l Arb. J.   (International Arbitration Journal)
Int'l J. Crim. & Penology   (International Journal of Criminology and Penology)
Int'l L.Q.   (International Law Quarterly)
Int'l Law.   (International Lawyer, The)
Iowa   (Iowa Reports)
Iowa L. Rev.   (Iowa Law Review)
JAG J.   (JAG Journal)
J.A.M.A.   (Journal of the American Medical Association)
J. Am. Jud. Soc'y   (Journal of the American Judicature Society)
J. Bus. L.   (Journal of Business Law)
J. Can. B. Ass'n   (Journal of the Canadian Bar Association)
J. Crim. L.C. & P.S.   (Journal of Criminal Law, Criminology and Police Science)
J. Fam. L.   (Journal of Family Law)
J. For. Med.   (Journal of Forensic Medicine)
J. For. Sci.   (Journal of Forensic Sciences)
J. Int'l L. & Pol.   (Journal of International Law and Politics)
J. Legal Ed.   (Journal of Legal Education)
J. Mo. Bar   (Journal of the Missouri Bar)
J. Pat. Off. Soc'y   (Journal of the Patent Office Society)
J. Pub. L.   (Journal of Public Law)
Judge Advoc. J.   (Judge Advocate Journal, The)
Judge's J.   (Judge's Journal)
Jurid. Rev.   (Juridical Review)
Jurimetrics J.   (Jurimetrics Journal)
Juv. Ct. J.   (Juvenile Court Journal)

K.B.   (Law Reports King's Bench (Eng.)
Kan.   (Kansas Reports)
Ky.   (Kentucky Reports)
Ky. L.J.   (Kentucky Law Journal)

L. Ed.   (Lawyers' Edition, U.S. Supreme Court Reports)
L. Ed.2d   (Lawyers' Edition, U.S. Supreme Court Reports, Second Series)
L. Inst. J.   (Law Institute Journal)
L.Q. Rev.   (Law Quarterly Review)
L.R.A.   (Lawyers Reports Annotated)
L.R.A. (n.s.)   (Lawyers Reports Annotated, New Series)

La.   (Louisiana Supreme Court Reports)
La. App.   (Louisiana Courts of Appeal Reports)
Lab. Arb.   (Labor Arbitration Reports (BNA)
La. B.J.   (Louisiana Bar Journal)
L.A. Bar Ass'n Bull.   (Los Angeles Bar Association Bulletin)
Lab. L.J.   (Labor Law Journal)
La. L. Rev.   (Louisiana Law Review)
Lab. Rel. Rep.   (Labor Relations Reporter (BNA)
Land & Water L. Rev.   (Land and Water Law Review)
Law Soc'y Gaz.   (Law Society Gazette)
Lawyers' Med. J.   (Lawyers' Medical Journal)
Lincoln L. Rev.   (Lincoln Law Review)
Lloyd's List L.R.   (Lloyd's List Law Reports)
Low. Can. L.J.   (Lower Canada Law Journal)
Loyola L. Rev.   (Loyola Law Review)
Loyola U. Chi. L.J.   (Loyola University of Chicago Law Journal)
Loyola U.L.A.L. Rev.   (Loyola University of Los Angeles Law Review)

McGill L.J.   (McGill Law Journal)
Maine L. Rev.   (Maine Law Review)
Mar. L. Cas. (n.s.)   (Maritime Law Cases, New Series)
Marq. L. Rev.   (Marquette Law Review)
Mass.   (Massachusetts Reports)
Mass. App. Div.   (Massachusetts Appellate Division Reports)
Mass. L.Q.   (Massachusetts Law Quarterly)
Md.   (Maryland Reports)
Md. B.J.   (Maryland Bar Journal)
Md. L. Rev.   (Maryland Law Review)
Me.   (Maine Reports)
Med.-Legal J.   (Medico-Legal Journal)
Mercer L. Rev.   (Mercer Law Review)
Miami L.Q.   (Miami Law Quarterly)
Mich.   (Michigan Reports)
Mich. L. Rev.   (Michigan Law Review)
Mich. St. B.J.   (Michigan State Bar Journal)
Mil. L. Rev.   (Military Law Review)
Minn.   (Minnesota Reports)
Minn. L. Rev.   (Minnesota Law Review)
Misc.   (Miscellaneous (N.Y.)
Miss.   (Mississippi Reports)
Miss. L.J.   (Mississippi Law Journal)
Mo.   (Missouri Reports)
Mo. App.   (Missouri Appeal Reports)
Mo. B.J.   (Missouri Bar Journal)
Mo. L. Rev.   (Missouri Law Review)

Mod. L. Rev.   (Modern Law Review)
Mont.   (Montana Reports)
Mont. L. Rev.   (Montana Law Review)

NACCA L.J.   (NACCA Law Journal)
N.C.   (North Carolina Reports)
N.C. Cent. L.J.   (North Carolina Central Law Journal)
N.C. L. Rev.   (North Carolina Law Review)
N.D.   (North Dakota Reports)
N.E.   (North Eastern Reporter)
N.E.2d   (North Eastern Reporter, Second Series)
N.H.   (New Hampshire Reports)
N.H.B.J.   (New Hampshire Bar Journal)
N.J.   (New Jersey Reports)
N.J. Eq.   (New Jersey Equity Reports)
N.J. Misc.   (New Jersey Miscellaneous Reports)
N.J. Super.   (New Jersey Superior Court Reports)
N.L.R.B.   (National Labor Relations Board Decisions)
N.M.   (New Mexico Reports)
N. Mex. L. Rev.   (New Mexico Law Review)
N.W.   (North Western Reporter)
N.W.2d   (North Western Reporter, Second Series)
N.Y.   (New York Court of Appeals Reports)
N.Y. County Law. Ass'n B. Bull.   (New York County Lawyers Association
                                        Bar Bulletin)
N.Y. Crim.   (New York Criminal Reports)
N.Y. Jur.   (New York Jurisprudence)
N.Y. Misc.   (New York Miscellaneous Reports)
N.Y. Misc. 2d.   (New York Miscellaneous Second Series)
N.Y.S.   (New York Supplement)
N.Y.S.2d   (New York Supplement, Second Series)
N.Y. St. B.J.   (New York State Bar Journal)
N.Y.U.L. Rev.   (New York University Law Review)
N.Z.L.J.   (New Zealand Law Journal)
N.Z.L.R.   (New Zealand Law Reports)
Natural L.F.   (Natural Law Forum)
Natural Resources J.   (Natural Resources Journal)
Neb.   (Nebraska Reports)
Neb. L. Rev.   (Nebraska Law Review)
Negl. & Comp. Cas. Ann. 3d   (Negligence & Compensation Cases Annotated
                                    Third Series)
Negl. Cas.   (Negligence Cases (CCH)
Nev.   (Nevada Reports)
Notre Dame Law.   (Notre Dame Lawyer)

Nw. U.L. Rev.   (Northwestern University Law Review)

Ohio   (Ohio Reports)
Ohio App.   (Ohio Appellate Reports)
Ohio App. 2d   (Ohio Appellate Reports, Second Series)
Ohio Ct. App.   (Ohio Courts of Appeals Reports)
Ohio Dec.   (Ohio Decisions)
Ohio Op.   (Ohio Opinions)
Ohio Op. 2d   (Ohio Opinions, Second Series)
Ohio St.   (Ohio State Reports)
Ohio St. 2d   (Ohio State Reports, Second Series)
Oil & Gas Tax Q.   (Oil and Gas Tax Quarterly)
Okla.   (Oklahoma Reports)
Okla. L. Rev.   (Oklahoma Law Review)
Ore.   (Oregon Reports)
Ore. L. Rev.   (Oregon Law Review)
Osgoode Hall L.J.   (Osgoode Hall Law Journal)

P.   (Pacific Reporter)
P.2d   (Pacific Reporter, Second Series)
P. & F. Radio Reg.   (Radio Regulation Reporter)
P.R.F.   (Puerto Rico Federal Reports)
P.R.R.   (Puerto Rico Reports)
P.U.R.   (Public Utilities Reports)
P.U.R. (n.s.)   (Public Utilities Reports, New Series)
P.U.R.3d   (Public Utilities Reports, Third Series)
Pa.   (Pennsylvania State Reports)
Pa. County Ct.   (Pennsylvania County Court Reports)
Pa. D. & C.   (Pennsylvania District and County Reports)
Pa. D. & C. 2d   (Pennsylvania District and County Reports, Second Series)
Pa. Dist.   (Pennsylvania District Reports)
Pa. Misc.   (Pennsylvania Miscellaneous Reports)
Pa. Super.   (Pennsylvania Superior Court Reports)
Pat. T.M. & Copy. J.   (Patent, Trademark & Copyright Journal)
Police L.Q.   (Police Law Quarterly)
Pol. Sci. Q.   (Political Science Quarterly)
Pollution Abs.   (Pollution Abstracts)

Q.L.J.   (Queen's Law Journal)

R.I.   (Rhode Island Reports)
R.I.B.J.   (Rhode Island Bar Journal)
R.P.C.   (Reports of Patent Cases)
Race Rel. L. Rep.   (Race Relations Law Reporter)

Real Est. L. Rep.   (Real Estate Law Report)
Real Est. Rev.   (Real Estate Review)
Real Prop. Prob. & Trust J.   (Real Property, Probate and Trust Journal)
Record of N.Y.C.B.A.   (Record of the Association of the Bar of the City of
                        New York)
Restric. Prac.   (Reports of Restrictive Practices Cases)
Rev. C. Abo. P.R.   (Revista de Derecho del Colegio de Abogados de Puerto Rico)
Rev. Jur. U.P.R.   (Revista Juridica de la Universidad de Puerto Rico)
Rev. Bar.   (Revue du Barreau)
Rev. Legale   (Revue Legale)
Rev. Not.   (Revue de Notariat)
Rocky Mt. L. Rev.   (Rocky Mountain Law Review)
Rocky Mt. Min. L. Inst.   (Rocky Mountain Mineral Law Institute)
Rocky Mt. Mineral L. Rev.   (Rocky Mountain Mineral Law Review)
Rutgers-Camden L.J.   (Rutgers-Camden Law Journal)
Rutgers J. Computers & Law   (Rutgers Journal of Computers and the Law)
Rutgers L. Rev.   (Rutgers Law Review)

S. Afr. L.J.   (South African Law Journal)
S.C.   (South Carolina Reports)
S.C.L.Q.   (South Carolina Law Quarterly)
S.C.L. Rev.   (South Carolina Law Review)
S. Cal. L. Rev.   (Southern California Law Review)
S. Ct.   (Supreme Court Reporter)
S.D.   (South Dakota Reports)
S.D.L. Rev.   (South Dakota Law Review)
S.D. St. B.J.   (South Dakota State Bar Journal)
S.E.   (South Eastern Reporter)
S.E.2d   (South Eastern Reporter, Second Series)
S.E.C.   (Securities and Exchange Commission Decisions and Reports)
S. Tex. L.J.   (South Texas Law Journal)
S.W.   (South Western Reporter)
S.W.2d   (South Western Reporter, Second Series)
San Diego L. Rev.   (San Diego Law Review)
Santa Clara Law.   (Santa Clara Lawyer)
Scots L.T.R.   (Scots Law Times Reports)
Sec. L. Rev.   (Securities Law Review)
Sel. Serv. L. Rptr.   (Selective Service Law Reporter)
Seton Hall L. Rev.   (Seton Hall Law Review)
So.   (Southern Reporter)
So.2d   (Southern Reporter, Second Series)
Sol. J.   (Solicitors' Journal)
St. John's L. Rev.   (St. John's Law Review)
St. Louis U.L.J.   (Saint Louis University Law Journal)

St. Mary's L.J.   (St. Mary's Law Journal)
Stan. L. Rev.   (Stanford Law Review)
Student Law. J.   (Student Lawyer Journal)
Suffolk U.L. Rev.   (Suffolk University Law Review)
Sw. L.J.   (Southwestern Law Journal)
Sw. U.L. Rev.   (Southwestern University Law Review)
Syracuse L. Rev.   (Syracuse Law Review)

T. Bull.   (Treasury Bulletin)
Tax A.B.C.   (Tax Appeal Board Cases)
Tax Adviser   (Tax Adviser, The)
Tax Cas.   (Tax Cases)
Tax Counselor's Q.   (Tax Counselor's Quarterly)
Tax L. Rev.   (Tax Law Review)
Tax. Law.   (Tax Lawyer, The)
Taxes   (Taxes, the Tax Magazine)
Temp. L.Q.   (Temple Law Quarterly)
Tenn.   (Tennessee Reports)
Tenn. App.   (Tennessee Appeals Reports)
Tenn. L. Rev.   (Tennessee Law Review)
Tex.   (Texas Reports)
Tex. B.J.   (Texas Bar Journal)
Tex. Civ. App.   (Texas Civil Appeals Reports)
Tex. Crim.   (Texas Criminal Reports)
Tex. Jur.   (Texas Jurisprudence)
Tex. Jur.2d   (Texas Jurisprudence, Second Series)
Texas L. Rev.   (Texas Law Review)
Tex. So. U.L. Rev.   (Texas Southern University Law Review)
Tex. Tech L. Rev.   (Texas Tech Law Review)
Trade Cas.   (Trade Cases (CCH)
Trade Reg. Rep.   (Trade Regulation Reporter (CCH)
Trademark Rptr.   (Trade-Mark Reporter)
Transp. L.J.   (Transportation Law Journal)
Trial Judges' J.   (Trial Judges' Journal)
Trial Law. Guide   (Trial Lawyers' Guide)
Trusts & Estates   (Trusts and Estates)
Tul. L. Rev.   (Tulane Law Review)
Tul. Tax. Inst.   (Tulane Tax Institute)
Tulsa L.J.   (Tulsa Law Journal)

U.C.D.L. Rev.   (University of California at Davis Law Review)
U.C.L.A. Intra. L. Rev.   (U.C.L.A. Intra. L. Rev.)
U.C.L.A.L. Rev.   (U.C.L.A. Law Review)
U.C.L.A.-Alaska L.   (U.C.L.A.-Alaska Law Review)

U. Chi. L. Rev.   (University of Chicago Law Review)
U. Chi. L. Rec.   (University of Chicago Law School Record)
U. Cin. L. Rev.   (University of Cincinnati Law Review)
U. Colo. L. Rev.   (University of Colorado Law Review)
U. Det. L.J.   (University of Detroit Law Journal)
U. Fla. L. Rev.   (University of Florida Law Review)
U. Ill. L.F.   (University of Illinois Law Forum)
U. Kan. City L. Rev.   (University of Kansas City Law Review)
U. Kan. L. Rev.   (University of Kansas Law Review)
U. Miami L. Rev.   (University of Miami Law Review)
U. Mich. J. Law   (University of Michigan Journal of Law Reform)
U. Mo. Bull. L. Ser.   (University of Missouri Bulletin Law Series)
U. Mo. K.C.L. Rev.   (University of Missouri at Kansas City Law Review)
U.N.B.L.J.   (University of New Brunswick Law Journal)
U. Pa. L. Rev.   (University of Pennsylvania Law Review)
U. Pitt. L. Rev.   (University of Pittsburgh Law Review)
U. Queens L.J.   (University of Queensland Law Journal)
U. Rich. L. Rev.   (University of Richmond Law Review)
U.S.   (United States Supreme Court Reports)
U.S. Av.   (United States Aviation Reports)
U.S.C.   (United States Code)
U.S.C. (Supp.)   (United States Code Supplement)
U.S.C.A.   (United States Code Annotated)
U.S.C.M.A.   (United States Court of Military Appeals)
U.S. Code Cong. & Ad. News   (United States Code Congressional and
                                 Administrative News)
U.S.C.S.   (United States Code Service)
U.S.L.W.   (United States Law Week (B.N.A.)
U.S.P.Q.   (United States Patent Quarterly)
U.S. Tax Cas.   (United States Tax Cases (CCH)
U. San Fernando V.L. Rev.   (University of San Fernando Valley Law Review)
U. San Fran. L. Rev.   (University of San Francisco Law Review)
U. Toledo L. Rev.   (University of Toledo Law Review)
U. Toronto L.J.   (University of Toronto Law Journal)
U. Tor. L. Rev.   (University of Toronto School of Law Review
U.W. Austl. L. Rev.   (University of Western Australia Law Review)
U.W.L.A.L. Rev.   (University of West Los Angeles School of Law, Law Revi
U. Wash. L. Rev.   (University of Washington Law Review)
Un. Prac. News   (Unauthorized Practice News)
Urban Law Ann.   (Urban Law Annual)
Urban Law.   (Urban Lawyer, The)
Utah L. Rev.   (Utah Law Review)
Utah   (Utah Reports)
Utah 2d   (Utah Reports, 2d Series)

Util. L. Rep.   (Utilities Law Reporter (CCH)

V.I.   (Virgin Islands Reports)
V.I.B.J.   (Virgin Islands Bar Journal)
Va.   (Virginia Reports)
Va. Bar News   (Virginia Bar News)
Va. J. Int'l L.   (Virginia Journal of International Law)
Va. L. Rev.   (Virginia Law Review)
Val. U.L. Rev.   (Valparaiso University Law Review)
Vand. J. Transnat'l L.   (Vanderbilt Journal of Transnational Law)
Vt.   (Vermont Reports)
Vict. U. Well. L. Rev.   (Victoria University of Wellington Law Review)
Vill. L. Rev.   (Villanova Law Review)

W. Ont. L. Rev.   (Western Ontario Law Review)
W. Res. L. Rev.   (Western Reserve Law Review)
W. Va.   (West Virginia Reports)
W. Va. L. Rev.   (West Virginia Law Review)
Wage & Hour Cas.   (Wage and Hour Cases (BNA)
Wake For. Intra. L. Rev.   (Wake Forest Intramural Law Review)
Wake For. L. Rev.   (Wake Forest Law Review)
Wash.   (Washington Reports)
Wash.2d   (Washington Reports, Second Series)
Wash. & Lee L. Rev.   (Washington and Lee Law Review)
Wash. L. Rev.   (Washington Law Review)
Wash. U. L.Q.   (Washington University Law Quarterly)
Washburn L.J.   (Washburn Law Journal)
Wayne L. Rev.   (Wayne Law Review)
Willamette L.J.   (Willamette Law Journal)
Wisc.   (Wisconsin Reports)
Wis. L. Rev.   (Wisconsin Law Review)
Wisc. Stud. B.J.   (Wisconsin Student Bar Journal)
Wm. & Mary L. Rev.   (William & Mary Law Review)
Women Law. J.   (Women Lawyer's Journal)
Workmen's Comp. L. Rev. (Lloyd's)   (Workmen's Compensation Law Review,
                                      Lloyd's)
Wyo.   (Wyoming Reports)
Wyo. L.J.   (Wyoming Law Journal)

Yale L.J.   (Yale Law Journal)
Yale Rev. Law & Soc. Act'n   (Yale Review of Law and Social Action)

Appendix E

USING SHEPARD'S CITATIONS

The following is excerpted from the very helpful publication, "How To Use Shepard's Citations," with permission of the publisher, Shepard's Citations, Inc., Colorado Springs, Colorado, copyrighted 1971. Complimentary copies of their publication are available from the publisher or at major law libraries.

Every set of reports in a working library should have the corresponding Shepard unit alongside. Shepard's Citations will:

Locate additional authorities.
Evaluate the authority.
Pinpoint the search to the point of law under consideration.

The Shepard publications are designed to work with all methods of legal research and can be used effectively with:

Digests — Reports
Constitutions, Codes, Statutes
Text books — Encyclopedias
Ordinances and Court Rules
Law Reviews
"Loose leaf" Services

By checking every case found in an annotated code, digest, encyclopedia or text book through the appropriate Shepard publication, the Shepard system gives the investigator, with unvarying consistency, the complete judicial history and interpretation of every reported case as affected by the decisions of every state and federal court, thereby showing the present-day weight and value of the case as authority with the exceptions, limitations, etc. that may have been engrafted upon it. *In checking specific cases through the case divisions of Shepard's Citations it will become increasingly apparent that many later and additional cases will almost invariably be discovered that would not be disclosed by any other system of legal research.*

The same thing is equally true of the statutory divisions which within the scope of a particular Shepard publication show not only the legislative history of a statute but all of the cases citing a statute. In these divisions the interpretation or construction of an article, title or section of a constitutional or statutory provision by a state or federal court or the effect of a subsequent act of Congress or other legislative body may be immediately observed.

In studying the illustrations provided, one will observe that Shepard citation books, being compiled differently from all other law books, produce results for the investigator that are not to be obtained from any other method of legal research. When Shepard's Citations presents a list of cases as having cited a particular case or statute, that list is not the result of an editor's opinion but is a listing of cases which *physically cite* the particular case or statute. *It is a list which the courts themselves have created.* Every case is one in which the court has taken away from or given to the cited case or statute some element of force, weight or scope which theretofore the particular case or statute did not have.

Important Points to Be Observed in Using
Shepard's Citations to Cases

1. Select the reported decision in point with your case or the reported decision announcing the principle you wish to investigate.

2. Select the headnote or syllabus paragraph of that reported decision containing the principle applicable to the matter before you.

3. In the appropriate Shepard bound volume or volumes locate the volume number of the reports on the upper outside corner of the page.

4. Then examine the columns below for the bold face type numbers which indicate the initial page of the reports on which the decision under investigation is reported.

5. The citations following the bold face type numbers indicate on the left the volume and on the right the page of the reports where the decision under investigation is cited.

6. Examine the letter-form abbreviations preceding the citing reference to ascertain whether or not the cited case has been *affirmed, reversed, dismissed, etc.* or *criticised, distinguished, etc.*

7. Note the small superior figures to the left of the page numbers of any citing references. These correspond to the number of the paragraph of the syllabus or headnote of the case under investigation which states the principle of law involved in the citing case.

8. After locating all of the citing cases in the Shepard bound volume or volumes, refer to the current issue of the paper-covered cumulative supplement and any current advance sheet and proceed in the same manner.

9. Then in turn trace in the appropriate Shepard publication the history and treatment of any particularly pertinent case or statute which has cited or construed the case under consideration.

Shepard's United States Citations
Case Edition

Vol. 396 — UNITED STATES SUPREME COURT REPORTS

—64—	—77—	—122—	—162—	—226—	—435—	—471—	—490—
(24LE264)	(24LE275)	(24LE312)	(24LE340)	(24LE382)	(24LE634)	(24LE663)	(24LE699)
(90SC355)	(90SC363)	(90SC337)	(90SC309)	s396US19	(90SC628)	(90SC671)	(90SC707)
s238F2d657	s298FS1260	s400F2d548	s294FS1103	s419F2d1212	s220Ga280	s391F2d586	—191—
s243F2d837	f422F2d¹162	s274FS449	s312FS442	cc417F2d801	s224Ga826	s299FS1389	(24LE700)
s265F2d9	424F2d1295	422F2d²930	s331ICC447	d420F2d⁴548	s138SE573	397US¹820	(90SC708)
s403F2d340	426F2d⁴986	422F2d⁶507	s333ICC720	f421F2d¹122	s165SE160	398US431	s296FS853
f396US479	428F2d105	d425F2d⁴340	397US⁴606	f421F2d¹135	cc382US326	d399US¹387	s328ICC460
j396US84	428F2d²106	d425F2d²²46	421F2d¹780	f421F2d¹137	cc221Ga870	428F2d552	s331ICC228
	428F²⁰¹111	49⁰⁰	⁹⁰FS¹	⁴⁰¹F²⁴¹¹⁰⁰	⁰¹⁴⁸SF⁰⁰	⁹⁰F²⁴611	⁰⁰⁰¹⁰⁰869

Vol. 24 — LAWYERS' EDITION, UNITED STATES SUPREME COURT REPORTS, 2d Series

—264—	—275—	—312—	—340—	—382—	—634—	—663—	—699—
(396US64)	(396US77)	(396US122)	(396US162)	(396US226)	(396US435)	(396US471)	(396US490)
s238F2d657	s298FS1260	US reh den	s294FS1103	s24LE19	s220Ga280	s391F2d586	—700—
s243F2d837	f422F2d⁶162	s274FS449	s312FS442	s419F2d1212	s224Ga826	s299FS1389	(396US491)
s265F2d9	424F2d	s400F2d548	s331ICC447	cc417F2d801	s138SE573	226	s296FS853
s403F2d340	⁶1295	s274FS449	s333ICC720	d420F2d⁴548	s165SE160	26LE³382	s328ICC460
24LE²278	426F2d⁴986	422F2d⁶30	25LE²607	f421F2d¹122	cc15LE373	26LE⁶382	s331ICC228
j24LE²81	428F2d¹105	422F2d⁶507	421F2d¹780	f421F2d¹135	cc221Ga870	d26LE⁶687	s331ICC869
419F2d⁴90	428F²⁴⁰	⁰⁰⁰⁴¹⁹⁴⁰	491F⁰⁰³⁸⁰	f49¹⁰⁰⁰	⁰⁰¹⁴⁸SF⁰⁰⁰	⁹⁰³F⁰⁰⁰⁸	⁰⁰²⁹⁹¹CC20⁶

Vol. 90 — SUPREME COURT REPORTER

—337—	—355—	—363—	—628—	—671—	—708—	—746—	—1026—
(396US122)	(396US64)	(396US77)	(396US435)	(396US471)	(396US491)	(396US	(397US280)
s400F2d548	s238F2d657	s298FS1260	s220Ga280	s391F2d586	s296FS853	1235)	s296FS138
s274FS449	s243F2d837	f422F2d²162	s224Ga826	s299FS1389	s328ICC460	—763—	cc90SC1028
422F2d⁶30	s265F2d9	424F2d1295	s138SE573	90SC1517	s331ICC228	(397US1)	90SC1017

113

National Reporter System
Illustration

To illustrate the use of Shepard's National Reporter Citations we will use the same case, Welch v. Swasey, that was selected to demonstrate the use of the state publication. This time we will make our search in terms of its Northeastern Reporter reference, 79 NE 745. The mechanics are the same as in the preceding illustration dealing with a state reports edition.

Let us further consider this Reporter citator in light of its use as a case finder. By a check of the specimen page (opposite) we find every Massachusetts case that cites 79 NE 745 in terms of their Northeastern Reporter references; cases from other states within the scope of the Northeastern Reporter, namely Illinois, Indiana, New York and Ohio. In addition, we find every other state citing reference to our case (nineteen states in addition to those within the Northeastern Reporter area). Add to this the references to annotations and you can see that exhaustive national research is instantly available, opening avenues of investigation that would have required countless hours of search using other methods.

The use of the Northeastern Reporter publication with respect to the evaluation of our material is also exactly the same as in the state reports example as is the ability to pinpoint research by use of the small superior figures immediately to the left of the page reference.

When research in depth is desired the careful investigator will use both the state and the Reporter citation units in searching his problem. The state units being intrastate in their orientation will emphasize local citing references, including statutory material and law reviews. The Reporter units, with their interstate frame of reference in addition to state case coverage, also lead to regional and national citing references.

NOTE: To obtain regional and national citing references for cases reported prior to the first units of the National Reporter System use your Shepard "State" edition.

								—776—
142NE¹694	127NE⁴528	161SE80	105NE¹985	N D	178NE¹542	113NE¹202		(193Mas402)
Ind	135NE³876	N H	105NE²987	137NW416	181NE¹219	h124NE431		f80NE¹807
96NE¹977	136NE²339	141At145	127NE¹432	Nebr	d186NE¹671	d131NE¹855		81NE¹911
107AR23n	136NE⁴339	Okla	140NE¹594	180NW560	188NE¹391	h142NE¹90		130NE³206
W Va	139NE382	192P353	189NE²593	N H	SNE¹781	142NE¹799		177NE²823
73SE268	f145NE²264	So C	26?				7	22NE¹146
—741—	145NE⁴268	150SE275	j70	Cited in annotations of the American			7	129AR13n
(193Mas545)	150NE⁴897	Va		Law Reports			30	Conn
—742—	153NE⁵336	67SE376	164So569	Okla	252F¹516	186F¹754		92At681
Case 1	161NE¹899	1348E916	Calif	138P155	N Y	**—770—**		Idaho
(193Mas398)	170NE¹391	192ES888	258P139	Ore	166NE¹174	(193Mas455)		26P2d122
182NE¹583	191NE¹35	Wis	Del	206P297	50AR1366n	98NE¹696		Me
Iowa	193NE815	147NW28	197At384	S D	Ark	116NE¹544		104At228
179NW528	f41F2d¹938	194NW161				NE¹112		(193Mas378)
—742—	Ill	196NW455		Followed with reference to para-		NE179		**—777—**
Case 2	e04NE²924	W Va		graph one of syllabus		NE¹351		124NE¹21
(193Mas359)	133NE⁵270	84SE107	s92NE61	Vt	20P2d752	197NE¹888		32AR215n
89NE¹133	149NE¹789	94SE498	81NE¹914	130At767	Conn	d14NE¹154		**—779—**
92NE¹1031	180NE¹773	**—748—**	f83NE¹1019	Wis	85At636	36NE¹413		Case 1
95NE¹400	193NE¹134	(193Mas431)	84NE¹8	196NW766	Del	48NE¹44		(194Mas44)
102NE²66	Ind	88NE³591	88NE¹696	W Va	197At486	(193Mas336)		104NE¹467
112NE²952	d92NE⁵650	f116NE¹899			Idaho		190	107NE²58
139NE³383	172NE¹312	56F2d²811		Cited by the lower federal courts			387	165NE²903
164NE376	172NE⁴312	Ill					237n	167NE¹679
172NE¹215	N Y	104NE¹675	**—757—**	**—763—**	Minn	**—772—**		191NE²103
3NE⁴27	118NE³792	177IIA181	(75OS855)	(193Mas486)	217NW375	(193Mas551)		N Y
266F²198	150NE¹123	154897	119NE¹416	s87NE189	Mo	99NE¹415		38S2d300
28FS²157	2168311	f104NE¹61	142NE²691	s90NE578	236SW20	100NE¹62		Ga
46FS⁴957	2208690	N Y	3NE²354	s94NE752	Okla	102NE¹420		23SE418
41AR127n	2588890	119NE¹558	30A496	92NE¹47	159P1013	137NE²375		**—779—**
44AR1068n	14S2d503	217859	90A22	108NE¹1086	Va	137NE¹694		Case 2
126AR1095n	28S2d318	Me	Ind	33NE¹269	63SE448	156NE¹744		(193Mas540)
126AR1097n	Ohio	108At194	e89NE¹517	**—764—**	86SE66	161NE¹621		87NE762
Ala	149NE⁴33	Mo	e89NE³517	(193Mas507)	128SE541	192NE¹630		21AR1445n
70So728	34AR46n	164SW641	**—762—**	80NE¹508	1628E20	10NE¹126		**—780—**
169So719	Ala	**—749—**	(193Mas556)	80NE¹697	Wash	36FS¹925		Case 1
Ark	52So945	Case 1	102NE¹67	81NE²888	5P2986	36FS¹928		(193Mas593)
65SW15	Calif	(193Mas331)	d155NE¹443	82NE¹497	**—766—**	Ill		106NE³852
Calif	134P973	Conn	165NE¹513	84NE¹842	(193Mas419)	101NE¹945		138NE²7
55P2d228	Conn	85NE¹847	j169NE¹493	86NE²936	88NE¹836	N Y		138NE¹816
Ga	111At357	108NE¹364	181NE¹716	87NE613	f93NE¹605	2888440		144NE²764
86SE328	111At902	**—749—**	15NE¹487	92NE²720	f95NE¹94	Ohio		196NE860
Miss	162At29	Case 2	232F²559	94NE¹390	96NE¹1005	142NE¹896		199NE²896
80So282	165At605	(193Mas438)	296F²375	104NE¹381	100NE¹557	Me		42NE¹562
Tenn	179At200	79NE¹751	Ill	107NE450	f128NE¹14	145At398		21AR1459n
192SW169	Del	87NE¹475	241IIA17	152NE¹78	152NE¹578	N J		60AR385n
—744—	129At518	f8			69	8A2d569		Ala
(194Mas47)	Fla		Cited in all units of the National Re-			**—774—**		16180551
121NE¹31	658284		porter System with state of citing		18	(193Mas400)		Pa
158NE¹799	948o689		case shown			89NE¹546		162At344
Vt	157So655	98			**—765—**	104NE¹450		Tex
13A2d208	Iowa	117NE¹311	108AR411n	(193Mas332)	22AR578n	138NE¹551		252SW268
Wyo	126NW917	136NE¹104	108AR419n	81NE¹895	Ala	145NE¹54		**—780—**
120P2d597	184NW830	19AR1372n	108AR421n	85NE¹571	81So21	152NE¹229		Case 2
—745—	273		Ala	NE¹573	Ark	152NE¹229		(193Mas534)
(193Mas364)		Cross references to state reports		NE¹490	179SW818	169NE¹517		106NE¹633
a214US91	46F			NE²564	Conn	187NE¹107		108NE¹471
a53LE923	Ky		101P2d715	90NE¹534	181At209	32NE¹271		127NE¹517
a298C567	198W975	Minn	Iowa	90NE¹548	Iowa	**—775—**		137NE¹295
f79NE¹879	M	209NW240			186NW442	Case 1		144NE¹404
84NE⁵456	70At114		Affirmed "a" by the United States		Ky	(193Mas453)		146NE¹687
86NE¹917	95At1063		Supreme Court		78W228	97NE¹100		177NE¹270
d89NE¹146	Me			Kan	109NE⁵85	110NE¹962		e31NE⁴554
80NE³180	69At629	85NE¹573	171P6	107NE¹377	N D	135NE¹189		235F¹653
92NE¹708	128At185	93NE¹840	Md	112NE¹1025	147NW785	Utah		65F2d¹868
f92NE⁴709	137At400	95NE¹752	96At518	134NE²376	R I	220P699		N Y
94NE³1045	140At387	120NE¹591	Me	139NE¹822	129At804	**—775—**		2908212
95NE⁵932	Minn	142NE¹904	138At71	141NE¹587	So C	Case 2		56AR65n
106NE⁵853	158	168NE¹632		157NE¹652	768E699	(193Mas518)		Vt
107NE3?9		Citations analyzed to paragraph of				59	92NE506	146At74
111NE⁵412		syllabus of cited case				98	228NW507	(193Mas500)
114NE⁵289	25					634	94NE²266	**—781—**
117NE⁵588	256SW491	97NE²103	135SW73	f168NE172	(193Mas444)	97NE¹921		88NE¹334
119NE⁵689	N C	100NE²545	N C	169NE¹781	90NE¹590	190NE²737		**Continued**
127NE¹527	122SE472	e104NE¹344	195SE808	177NE¹580	94NE¹466			

For later citations see any subsequent bound supplement or volume, the current issue of the periodically published paper-covered cumulative supplement and any current issue of the advance sheet   1365

115